LITTLE
LOST SISTER

VIRGINIA BROOKS

1st WORLD
LIBRARY
Literary Society

Little Lost Sister

Virginia Brooks

© 1st World Library, 2009
PO Box 2211
Fairfield, IA 52556
www.1stworldlibrary.com
First Edition

LCCN: 2009923516

Softcover ISBN: 978-1-4218-8889-7
Hardcover ISBN: 978-1-4218-8988-7
eBook ISBN: 978-1-4218-8790-6

Purchase *"Little Lost Sister"*
as a traditional bound book at:
www.1stWorldLibrary.com/purchase.asp?ISBN=978-1-4218-8889-7

1st World Library is a literary, educational organization
dedicated to:

- Creating a free internet library of downloadable ebooks

- Hosting writing competitions and offering book publishing
scholarships.

Interested in more 1st World Library books? contact:
literacy@1stworldlibrary.com
Check us out at: www.1stworldlibrary.com

1ˢᵗ World Library Literary Society

Giving Back to the World

"If you want to work on the core problem, it's early school literacy."

- James Barksdale, former CEO of Netscape

"No skill is more crucial to the future of a child, or to a democratic and prosperous society, than literacy."

- Los Angeles Times

"Literacy... means far more than learning how to read and write... The aim is to transmit... knowledge and promote social participation."

- UNESCO

"Literacy is not a luxury, it is a right and a responsibility. If our world is to meet the challenges of the twenty-first century we must harness the energy and creativity of all our citizens."

- President Bill Clinton

"Parents should be encouraged to read to their children, and teachers should be equipped with all available techniques for teaching literacy, so the varying needs and capacities of individual kids can be taken into account."

- Hugh Mackay

CONTENTS

PROLOGUE

They came up suddenly over a bit of rising ground, the mill-owner and his friend the writer and student of modern industries, and stood in full view of the factory. The air was sweet with scent of apple-blossoms. A song sparrow trilled in the poplar tree.

"What do you think of our factory?" asked the man of business and of success, turning his keen, aggressive face towards his companion.

The other, the dreamer, waited for moments without speaking, carefully weighing the word, then he answered,

"Horrible."

"My dear fellow!" The owner's voice showed that he was really grieved. "Why horrible?"

"Your mill is a crime against Nature. Look how it violates that landscape. Look how it stands there gaunt and tawdry against these fresh green meadows edged round with billowy white clouds that herald summer. And you are proud of it. Could you not have found some arid waste for this factory? Can't you see how Nature cries out against this outrage? Can't you see that she has dedicated this country to seed-time and harvest,—these verdant fields, deep woods and brooding streams?"

"The Millville people wanted our factory. They paid us a subsidy to bring it here."

"Blind, too!" The dreamer looked backward at the town. "They tell me that the founders there called their village Farmington. Have you ever reflected what a change you are working in the lives of these people by substituting industrialism for agriculture? Have you thought of the moral transformations such a substitution must work among them?"

"We are not responsible for their morals," the mill-owner answered, impatiently. "We have spared nothing to make our factory up to date. The mill meets all the demands of modern hygiene and sanitation. We do that for them."

His friend was silent for a time.

"Your employes here are chiefly women, very young women," he said at last.

"Yes, we have two hundred girls," replied the mill-owner.

"What is your highest wage for a girl?"

"Eight dollars a week."

Again the younger man was silent. Then he took his friend's arm within his own.

"These girls are the mothers of tomorrow. To an extent the destinies of our race depend upon them. Your factory places upon you tremendous responsibilities."

Virginia Brooks

"We are growing to realize our responsibilities more and more," said the man of business and of success gravely. "Perhaps we do not realize them keenly enough. It is the fault of the times."

"Yes, it is the fault of the times. Life, honor, virtue itself trampled down in the rush for the dollar."

"I believe that a change is coming, though slowly. I believe that the day will come when we owners of mills will regard it as a disgraceful thing for our corporations to declare a dividend while notoriously underpaying our employes."

"Yes, and perhaps the day is coming, too, when the employer who maintains conditions in his mills that subtly undermine the virtue of his women workers will be regarded as a public enemy."

"No doubt, but that time is a long way ahead!"

"We must look to the future," said his friend. "We must work for the future, too!"

CHAPTER I

AT THE BUTTON MILL

Elsie Welcome was the one girl in the big machine room of the Millville button factory who did not rise when the bell sounded for the short afternoon recess. She swung on her revolving stool away from her machine and looked eagerly, thirstingly towards the windows where the other girls were crowding for breath of the fresh June air, but she did not stir to follow them. A resolution stronger than her own keen need of the recreation moments was singling out this young girl from among her two hundred companions, laughing and talking together.

"I will speak to Mr. Kemble now—now," she promised herself, watching for the foreman to enter the machine room, according to his daily custom at this hour. Elsie nerved herself to a task difficult to perform, even after her three years of work in the factory, even though she was one of the most skilful workers here.

She drew up her charmingly modeled little figure tensely, and held her small head high, her pure, beautiful features aglow with delicate color, her slender, shapely hands clasping and unclasping each other.

Virginia Brooks

The foreman came into the room. Elsie rose from her place and went to meet him, pushing back the pretty tendrils of her hair.

"Mr. Kemble," she said, "I should like to speak to you a moment."

Hiram Kemble was a tall, thin young man, deeply conscious of his own importance and responsibilities. He had risen by assiduous devotion to the details of button making from office boy to his present exalted state. His mind had become a mere filing cabinet for information concerning the button business.

He stood regarding the girl before him, feeling the attraction of her beauty and resenting it. He did not dislike her; he did not understand her, and it was his nature to distrust what he did not understand.

"Well," he said, with professional brusqueness, "what is it?"

"I wanted to ask you to—to—" Elsie hesitated, then went on with courage, "to raise my wages."

He looked at her in amazement, displeased. "How much are you getting now?"

"Only eight dollars a week."

"Only!" Hiram Kemble was satirical. "That's as much as the others are getting."

"I know it. But it's not enough. Our expenses are heavy. My mother has begun to—to—" Elsie choked. "My mother is compelled to take in washing. She's not strong enough for such heavy work."

"Your sister has a good job."

"She earns only nine dollars."

"Your father—"

Tears sprang to Elsie's eyes, but she would not let them fall. "He's not earning anything."

"I know." Kemble spoke accusingly. "He is drinking."

Elsie showed a flash of spirit: "That's not my fault!"

"Just so. But you can't hold the Millville Button Company responsible for your father's misbehavior."

"Is there any chance for me to get more pay?" There was a note of despair in her question.

"Not the least chance in the world. You are getting our maximum wage for women. I couldn't raise your pay if I wanted to without being specially authorized to do so by our board of directors."

"And I can never earn—never get any more here?"

"No."

The minute hand of the electric clock pushed forward. Again a bell sounded. Two hundred American girls who had had a few moments' respite came trooping wearily back to their places at the machines.

At the clang of the bell Kemble walked up the room. Elsie went back to her place drooping; she wore a beaten air as if he had struck her visibly.

The girls on either hand spoke to her as they slipped into their places, but she did not hear them. Hours of swift work followed. The machines whirred and the deft hands of the girls flew. These button workers had nearly all been recruited from the district around Millville. With rare exceptions they were descendants of the hardy Americans who had founded the town while it was still called Farmington. The founders had passed away. The outside world had pressed around the village until its people longed to play a more active role in the world. It had seemed a great day when the button factory came, and the town name was changed to Millville.

Now these daughters of the strong elder race were factory workers. The world had been made better by an output of thousands of shiny new buttons when at last the six o'clock whistle blew on this bright June day.

Elsie Welcome got up from her machine and picked up her hat listlessly. She walked to a window and looked out. Suddenly animation came into her face. A young man waved a handkerchief from an automobile which spun by on the gray turnpike below the mill. Elsie waved her handkerchief in return.

Kemble, watching the girl from across the room, saw the episode. He hurried across to her, with the air of pouncing on a victim.

"We'll have none of that here, Miss Welcome," he said. "If you have to flirt, don't flirt on the company's premises."

She turned upon him indignantly. "I am not flirting! That gentleman is a friend of mine."

Kemble sneered. "Oh, he is a friend, is he? Where does a

factory girl like you meet men who ride in automobiles?"

Elsie flushed scarlet; she bit her quivering lips.

"Ashamed to tell where you met him, are you?"

"What do you mean?"

"I mean I'm responsible to my employers for the character of the girls I employ here."

Elsie looked her contempt of him. She laughed a little low scornful laugh which made Kemble thoroughly angry.

"Look here, my girl," he said. "You don't know when you're well off. You are too independent." His tone of anger roused her temper, but she held herself in leash and answered with cold politeness:

"Mr. Kemble, when I feel myself getting independent, the first thing I shall do will be to get away from the Millville button factory."

Kemble was ready to retreat now. The interview was getting beyond his expectation. Elsie was one of the company's fastest workers. He could not afford to have her throw up her place. He did not want to lose her.

"Oh, but you like the factory, Miss Welcome," he said in a suddenly pacific tone.

"Like—the—factory! I hate it," returned the girl, all her pent-up wrongs finding expression. "I hate the mill and everything about it. Do you suppose any girl could like the prospect of being bottled up in this hole year after year for eight dollars a week? Why, some day, Mr. Kemble, I expect to pay eight dollars for a hat, for just one hat."

"So that's it," said Kemble, "fine feathers, eh? I know, you're like a lot of other girls who have come and gone in this factory. You've heard of Chicago's bright lights and you want to singe your wings in them. Let me tell you something, my girl, girls in your position don't get eight dollar hats without paying for them and if they haven't got the money they give something else. They give—"

"Stop," ordered the girl. "You shan't say that to me. I don't believe it. You can't convince me that there isn't something better in life for a girl like me than Millville and eight dollars a week."

"I pity your ignorance," said Kemble, loftily.

"It's not ignorance to want something better than this," replied Elsie. "Why should you taunt me with ignorance, anyway? What do you know about the world? You're just a foreman in a little country mill and because you are satisfied with a narrow little life like that you think everyone else ought to be."

The truth in this goaded Kemble into violation of rule number twelve for button factory foremen which exhorts such employes to be polite to women workers.

"Why the devil don't you go to Chicago and be done with it then?" he demanded. "You're one of these people that has to learn by experience." He sneered at her. "Perhaps you can get your friend in the auto to take you. Why don't you try it?"

Tears rushed to the girl's eyes. She began fastening on her hat to conceal her emotion.

"I'm going to Chicago," she muttered, "just as soon as I am able. Nothing there can be much worse than being compelled to work in Millville under you. Good gracious," she added maliciously, after giving him a thorough inspection, "it's no use to stand here arguing with you."

With this taunt Miss Elsie gave her hat a final adjustment, then, leaving Mr. Hiram Kemble speechless with rage and injured dignity, she walked out of the factory door.

CHAPTER II

SEEING MILLVILLE

The distance from the Millville button factory to the corner of Main and Pine streets in Millville itself is, if you take the short cut through Nutting's Grove, as all sensible Millvillians do, a five minutes' walk. If the reader, touring Millville in search of the beginnings of this story, will make that journey in his imagination he will find himself standing on the rough board walk in front of John Price's general store.

From her eminence on the top of one of Mr. John Price's high stools Patience Welcome glanced up from the ledger over which she was toiling, put the blunt end of her pen into her mouth and looked out into the street drenched in sunshine. A half dozen farmers' horses, moored to the hitching rack in front of the store, threshed restlessly with their tails at enthusiastic banqueting flies, newborn into a world that seemed to be filled with juicy horses.

The scene did not interest Patience. Her glance went on across the street where an overdressed young man, just alighted from an automobile, stood surveying his surroundings. His eyes met hers. He removed his hat with an elaborate bow. The girl, a little piqued and a little amused, reached over very quietly and drew down the window curtain. Then she resumed operations on the ledger with the sharp end of the pen.

Patience Welcome, like her sister, was dark of hair and eyes. Her hair, too, had the quality of forming into tendrils about her cheeks which glowed with a happy, if not a robust, healthfulness. But there the resemblance ended. The two girls were widely different personalities. Elsie, the younger, was impetuous by nature, imaginative, and easily swept off her mental balance by her emotions. She was ambitious, too, and Millville did not please her. Patience, no less imaginative, perhaps, possessed a stronger hold upon herself. She admired her daring sister, but she was sensible of the dangers of such daring and did not imitate her. She possessed the great gift of contentedness. It colored all her thoughts, created pleasant places for her in what, to Elsie, seemed a desolate life; it made Millville not only a bearable but even a happy place to live in. Millville understood Patience and loved her; Elsie, being less understandable, was less popular.

It had been a busy day in John Price's store and Patience was entering in her books items from a pile of bills on the desk before her. It was five minutes after her usual leaving time, but the girl accepted extra duty with a cheerfulness that was part of her nature.

In the midst of her work there was a bustle at the back of the store. John Price, local merchant prince and owner of this establishment, had returned from the yard at the rear of the store where he had been superintending the storing of goods, arrived on the late afternoon train. He was a wiry little old man of sixty, abrupt, nervous, irritable and given to sharpness of speech which, he was profoundly convinced, hid from outside perception a heart given to unbusinesslike tenderness. He busied himself noisily about the shelves for a few minutes, then suddenly stuck his head through the door of the little office in which Patience was working.

"What," he said, "you here? Get out. Go home."

"I'll be through in a few minutes," rejoined Patience, without taking her eyes from her figures.

"Tush," said Mr. Price. "What are you trying to do, give me a bad name with my trade? People will think I'm a slave driver. Get out."

"In just a minute," smiled Patience.

"Go home, I say," almost shouted Price. He took off his alpaca coat and hung it on a nail. Then he stepped up suddenly behind Patience, took the pen deliberately from her hand and pushed her off the stool.

"Must I throw you out?" he demanded. "Must I? Must I, eh?"

He pointed towards the door.

"All right, Mr. Price," said Patience submissively, gathering up her bills and thrusting them into a drawer.

"Hurry," said Price. "You'll be late for your supper."

"No, I won't," returned Patience, putting on her jacket and hat. "This is wash day at our house. Supper is always late on wash day."

"Wash day, eh? Then you ought to be home helping your mother."

"Elsie will help mother," replied Patience quietly.

"Are you sure about that?" demanded Mr. Price.

"Of course, I'm sure, Mr. Price," said Patience, hurt.

"Well," said Mr. Price, "I'm not so sure. But don't stand here arguing. I haven't any time to argue with a snip of a girl like you. Get out. Go home!"

Patience, still a little hurt by her employer's expressed doubt about her sister, started for the front door. Looking out, she saw the overdressed young man with the automobile still standing across the street. He saw her, too, and waved his cigarette. Patience turned back into the store.

"Girl," demanded Mr. Price, his patience now seemingly exhausted, "where in the devil are you going?"

"Out the back way, if you please, Mr. Price."

Mr. Price got up deliberately from the stool which he had occupied as soon as Patience had vacated it and looked out of the front door.

"The young whelp," he said, apostrophizing the overdressed youth with the cigarette. Then to Patience: "Dodging him, eh? Now don't blush, girl. I don't blame him for looking at you. You're worth looking at. But you show mighty good sense in keeping away from him."

"Why, Mr. Price, I—" Patience stammered.

"O, that's all right, dodge him, keep him guessing. One of those freshies from the city, eh? Well, there's mighty little good in 'em. Give your ma my best regards. Tell her she's got a fine daughter. Good night."

Patience left the store by the rear door and started briskly for her home. She had gone but a block when she heard a wagon rumbling behind her and a voice called out:

"'Lo, there, Patience, late, ain't you?"

It was Harvey Spencer, ambitious "all round" clerk, hostler, collector for Millville's leading grocer. He drove a roan colt which went rather skittishly. There was an older man in the wagon with him. Harvey drew up the colt beside Patience with a vociferous "Whoa."

"Yes," replied Patience, "I'm a little late. Lots of business these days, Harvey?"

"You bet," he retorted, "Millville is flourishing. We'll soon have a real city here. Oh, Miss Welcome, let me make you acquainted with my friend, Mr. Michael Grogan of Chicago."

Patience accepted the introduction with flushed reserve.

"I'm right glad to know you," stated Mr. Grogan, removing his hat gallantly and wiping a perspiring brow with his handkerchief. "But let me tell you I don't think much of your friend, Harvey Spencer. Sure, I've been riding with him for two hours and you're the first pleasant object he's shown me. And such a ride! It's a certainty that this young fellow knows every bump and thank-ye-ma'am in the village and he's taken me full speed over all of them. I feel like I'd been churned. But I'll forgive him all that now—now that he's shown me you."

There was a sincerity in Mr. Grogan's raillery that swept away Patience's reserve. Besides, he was over fifty.

"Sure," she said, slyly imitating Mr. Grogan's brogue,

"you've been kissing the blarney stone, Mr. Grogan."

"Will ye listen to that now?" said Grogan enthusiastically, as he started to clamber off the wagon.

"Sit still, Mr. Grogan," said Harvey, laughing.

"But didn't you hear her, man alive? Sure, she's Irish—"

"No, I'm not," put in Patience, "but I've heard of the blarney stone."

"Look at that, now," said Grogan, returning to his seat with an air of keen disappointment. "And I was just longin' to see someone from the Ould Sod. I thought—"

"How do you like riding with Harvey?" inquired Patience, changing the subject.

"Well," said Grogan plaintively, "if I were twenty years younger maybe it would be good exercise, but with my years, Miss, 'tis just plain exhausting."

Here Harvey started the roan colt off again. "See you later," he called back to Patience, "I'm stopping at your house."

"So that's Tom Welcome's daughter, is it?" said Grogan as they got out of hearing.

"That's one of them," said Harvey, "but you ought to see the other."

"The old man now," went on Grogan, "is a good deal of a lush."

"The girls can't help what their father is," retorted Harvey, bridling.

"I know, I know," went on Mr. Grogan. "Such things happen in the best of families."

"No, and you can't blame Tom Welcome much, either," went on Harvey. "He was drove to drink. He invented an electrical machine that would have made a fortune for him and some one stole it from him. It wasn't the loss of the money that sent him to the devil, either. He'd spent a lifetime on his machine and just when he was getting it patented, some smart thief in Chicago takes it away from him. That's what I call tough luck."

"They're hard up, you say?" pursued Grogan.

Harvey, unconscious that he had said nothing of the sort, admitted that the Welcomes were in financial straits. "Their mother has to take in washing," he said, "and both the girls work. It's too bad, for they ought to be getting an education."

The roan colt came to an abrupt stop. They were in front of a small cottage. Grogan surveyed the place for a moment and then turned to his jehu. "And what might you be stopping here for?" he inquired.

Harvey paused with one foot on the step of the wagon and looked up at Grogan gravely.

"This is Tom Welcome's cottage," he said.

CHAPTER III

ENTER A DETECTIVE

While Harvey Spencer was climbing down from his wagon Mr. Michael Grogan, who was not exactly the guileless soul Millville took him to be, permitted himself rather a close inspection of the Welcome premises. There was nothing imposing about them. The cottage was old and obviously in need of repair. The fence which surrounded it had been repaired in places, apparently by someone who had small interest in the job. The little patch of ground in front, however, was decorated with a neatly kept vegetable garden bordered with flowers. The stone step at the cottage entrance was immaculate. Mr. Grogan was shrewd enough to indulge himself in the speculation that whatever Tom Welcome might be his wife was a careful housekeeper.

Mrs. Welcome was standing in her open door and Grogan studied her with a curiosity not entirely disinterested. Her figure was frail and slightly bowed. Her hair, as it showed in the deepening dusk was almost white. Her features had delicacy like those of the daughter Grogan had just met. She was wiping her hands on a gingham apron. They were hands of a hard working woman.

"Hello, Mrs. Welcome, nice day, ain't it?" called Harvey as

he came through the gate.

"Yes, it is nice, isn't it, Harvey?" replied Martha Welcome. "I hadn't noticed it before, I've been so busy with the washing."

The woman's voice, Mr. Grogan noted, held a note of sadness.

"Seems to me," said Harvey, dropping his voice and speaking with the assurance of an old family friend, "that if I had two girls like your Elsie and Patience, I'd see that they helped out with the washing."

"How can they help me?" replied Mrs. Welcome. "Patience is up early every morning and off to Mr. Price's store and Elsie is at the mill all day."

"That's so," said Harvey, "I didn't think, but surely they might—"

"Oh, they help a lot," broke in Mrs. Welcome, hurriedly. "They do all their ironing at night. And that's all anyone could ask of them after they come home tired from their work."

"Well, I'm glad to hear it. Your two girls always do look nice."

"Thank you, Harvey."

"But Mrs. Welcome—"

"Yes, Harvey?"

"Don't you think—" Harvey stopped and looked about hesitatingly,—"Ah, don't you think it would be just as well if

Elsie didn't see quite as much of this Chicago fellow?"

"Do you mean Mr. Druce?" inquired Mrs. Welcome.

"I do. Of course, he's all right—" Harvey again hesitated and puckered his lips thoughtfully. "He wears fine clothing, patent leather shoes, sports a diamond ring, but it seems to me Elsie's different somehow since that Martin Druce began to hang around."

Mrs. Welcome laughed softly. There was a glint of humor in her eyes. "I guess you're jealous, aren't you, Harvey?"

"Well, say I am," agreed Harvey. "Never mind that. Is it a good thing for Elsie?"

"Elsie's a good girl," replied Mrs. Welcome.

"She sure is, Mrs. Welcome. That's why I want her to be Mrs. Harvey Spencer."

Mrs. Welcome opened her eyes wide at this statement and looked kindly at the stout young man before her.

"You mean it, Harvey?" she demanded.

"I'm so much in earnest," he replied, fumbling in his pocket, "that I've got the ring right here."

He produced a plain gold wedding ring nestling in a white velvet case. Mrs. Welcome uttered a little cry of gladness. She believed in Harvey, who, incidentally, was all he pretended to be.

"O, I know I ain't much," went on Harvey, "just a clerk in a small town store, but I've got ambitions. Look at all the great men! Where did they begin? At the bottom."

Harvey paused. Then he looked all about him carefully and, satisfied with this survey, leaned confidentially toward Mrs. Welcome and whispered:

"Say, can you keep a secret, Mrs. Welcome?"

"I guess so," replied Mrs. Welcome smiling. "Try me, Harvey."

"All right, I'm going to be a detective," Harvey announced proudly.

"You are, Harvey?" was the astonished reply.

"Just watch me," Harvey went on. "I'm taking a correspondence school course. Here are some of my lessons." He took some closely typewritten sheets of paper from his pocket. "Ever notice how broad I am between the eyes?" he demanded.

"I can't say that I have," said Mrs. Welcome.

"Well, I am, and it's one of the signs, so they say, of the born detective. Listen here a moment."

He unfolded the bulky pages and read grandly:

"Always be observant of even the smallest trifles. A speck of dust may be an important clew to a murder."

"Harvey!" cried Mrs. Welcome.

"Don't be frightened, Mrs. Welcome, just wanted to show you that I mean business." Harvey paused for a moment and regarded her steadily. Then he pointed his finger at her accusingly as he said: "I knew you were washing before you told me!"

"You did, Harvey?"

"Sure, because you had suds on your apron where you dried your hands." He drew a deep sigh and threw out his chest. "There," he said. "Oh, I guess I'm bad at these lessons, eh?"

"You're a good boy, Harvey," replied Mrs. Welcome, indulgently.

"Thank you." He bowed. "Oh, perhaps my future mother-in-law and I aren't going to get along fine," he announced to the world in general, exultingly.

The roan colt interrupted this rhapsody by pawing impatiently at the ground. Harvey took his order book from his pocket and stuck his stub of lead pencil in his mouth.

"Well," he inquired, "how about orders, Mrs. Welcome?"

"We—we—need some flour," was the hesitating reply.

"A barrel?" suggested Harvey, turning to a fresh page of his order book.

"No—no—no—I—I guess ten pounds, and—I guess that's about all, Harvey."

"Now you'll excuse me if I doubt your word, Mrs. Welcome," said Harvey, writing down fifty pounds of flour quickly. "Come now, tell me what you do really want."

"O, what's the use. We need everything, we—" Mrs.

Welcome broke down and began to weep softly as she turned toward the house.

"Now hold on, Mrs. Welcome, don't break away from me like that!" Harvey followed her and laid his hand gently on her arm. "I hope Mr. Welcome isn't drinking again. Is he?"

"I'm afraid so, Harvey." Mrs. Welcome's frail shoulders quivered as she attempted to restrain her sobs. "Why, Tom hasn't been home for two days and—and our rent is due—and—"

Harvey Spencer interrupted with a prolonged whistle which seemed to be the best way he could think of expressing sympathy. A light dawned on him.

"That's why young Harry Boland is here from Chicago, to collect the rent, eh?" he inquired.

Mrs. Welcome nodded assent, "Yes," she said, "Mr. Boland has been very kind. He has waited two weeks and—and—we can't pay him."

"Why not let me—" suggested Harvey, putting his hand into his pocket. Mrs. Welcome checked him with a quick movement. "No, Harvey, please. I don't want you to do that," she said. "I wouldn't feel right about it somehow."

"Just as you say, Mrs. Welcome." Harvey was rather diffident and hesitated to press a loan on her. To change the subject he said: "Young Mr. Boland seems taken up with Patience."

"I hadn't noticed it," said Mrs. Welcome, drying her eyes.

"O, we detectives have to keep our eyes open," acclaimed

Harvey with another burst of pride.

But here Michael Grogan interrupted. "Young man," he called out from the roadway, "are you really taking orders or is this one of your visiting days?" He tied the colt and came into the yard.

"Hello," said Harvey, "getting tired of waiting?"

"Well, I felt myself growing to that hitching post," said Grogan, "so I tied that bunch of nerves you have out there and moved before I took root."

Harvey laughed and turned to Mrs. Welcome. "This is Mr. Michael Grogan, Mrs. Welcome," he said.

Mrs. Welcome backed away toward the porch, removing her apron. "Good afternoon, sir," she greeted him. "I hope you are well?"

"Well," said Grogan, "I was before this young marauder cajoled me into leaving me arm chair on the hotel veranda to go bumping over these roads."

Mrs. Welcome smiled and extended her hand. "I'm very glad to know you, Mr. Grogan. You mustn't mind Harvey's impetuous ways. He's all right here." She placed her hand on her heart.

"I'll go bail he is that if you say so, Mrs. Welcome," replied Grogan gallantly, "anyhow I'll take him on your word."

"Just ready to go, Mr. Grogan, when you called," put in Harvey. Then he caught Mrs. Welcome by the arm and bustled her into the house, saying: "And I'll see that you get all of those things, Mrs. Welcome, flour, corn meal, tomatoes, beans, lard—" and in spite of her protestations he closed the door on her with a parting: "Everything on the first delivery tomorrow morning sure." Then he added to Grogan, who stood smiling with a look of comprehension on his face, "All right. Ready to go."

"It's about time," commented Grogan as they went toward the wagon. "Don't think I'm too inquisitive if I ask who are these Welcomes anyhow?"

"People who are having a tough time," replied Harvey, unhitching his colt. "Tom Welcome used to be quite a man. He had that invention I was telling you about, an electric lamp. He was done out of it and went to the booze for consolation."

"So," murmured Grogan, half to himself, "Two girls in the family, eh?"

"Yes, that was one of them you met just before we came here."

"The pretty one?"

"Yes, and they're the best ever," added Harvey, antagonized by something he sensed in his companion's manner.

Grogan turned to him smiling. "There," he said, "don't get hot about it. Nobody doubts that, meself least of all. Ain't I Irish? It's the first article of every Irishman's creed to believe that all women, old or young, pretty or otherwise, all of them are just—good."

Harvey seized the older man's hand and shook it vigorously. Then looking up the road he said:

"Here comes Elsie Welcome, I think. I want you to meet her."

"Ah," retorted Grogan. He turned and looked at Elsie closely. She ran rapidly down the pathway toward the gate. She saw them, paused, walked more slowly and came up to them apparently in confusion.

"Why, hello Harv! What are you doing here so late?" she asked. Without waiting for a reply she started toward the gate flinging back a short "Good night."

The girl's whole manner indicated a guilty conscience. It was evident that she did not wish to talk to Harvey Spencer. She passed through the gate toward the door of her home.

CHAPTER IV

HARVEY MEETS "A DEALER IN CATTLE"

Harvey threw the reins into Grogan's lap and strode recklessly after Elsie. His good-natured face was flushed with anger.

"Say," he demanded, "what's the matter?"

The girl, unwilling, halted. "Nothing," she replied, "what makes you ask that?"

"Why," explained Harvey, hiding his anger and attempting to take her hand, "you're out of breath."

"Been running," was the girl's laconic explanation.

"You don't usually run home from the mill, Elsie," Harvey's detective instinct was showing itself.

Elsie was extremely irritated by this unwished for interview.

"Well, I—" she stammered, "I wanted to get here because it's Monday and mother's washing day and—" She paused, her irritation getting the better of her. "I don't see what right you have to question me, Harvey Spencer."

Grogan had got down from the wagon and at this moment came through the gate.

"Young man," he began, addressing Spencer. The girl interrupted him.

"Who are you?" she demanded. "Do you come from the mill?"

"I come from no mill," retorted Grogan, piqued by the girl's tone, "and if you'll excuse me I don't want to."

"This is Mr. Michael Grogan of Chicago," put in Harvey placatingly. "I've been showing him the town."

"And," added Grogan quickly, "I haven't seen much."

"That's not at all strange," said Elsie, "because there's nothing to see."

"And in Chicago, where I come from," said Grogan sagely, "there's altogether too much."

Grogan saw by his two companions' faces that he was an intruder.

"Young man," he said, "I don't think I'll wait for you. I've some letters to write at the hotel. I think I'll be strolling along."

"Why," said Harvey, hospitable in the face of intrusion, "you're welcome to ride. Won't you wait?"

"No, thanks," said Grogan, "that grocery wagon of yours wasn't built to accommodate a man of my size."

Harvey and the girl watched Grogan disappear in the dusk. Then the young man turned to the girl.

"Elsie—" he began tenderly.

But the girl stopped him. "Now don't begin to question me," she ordered. "I won't answer."

"You are trying to hide something from me," said Harvey, grasping the girl's unwilling hand. The girl drew away from him.

"That's not true," she said. "I don't want you to bother me."

"I never used to bother you," said Harvey, his face flushing.

"That was before—" began Elsie impulsively. "I mean now," she went on, catching herself. "I mean that you do now because you have changed."

"No," contradicted Harvey, "but you have."

"What do you mean by that?" challenged the girl.

Harvey stood silent for a moment and jerked out a laugh of embarrassment. "I don't know exactly what I mean," he said, "but you know we were engaged."

Elsie flushed. "We were not," she said.

"I mean," said Harvey miserably stumbling on, "we sort of were. We understood." He brought one hand from his pocket. It held the box containing the ring. "Why, Elsie," he said pleadingly, "I even bought the ring. Just a plain band of gold. I did so hope that some day, soon perhaps, you'd let me put it on your finger and take you to our home. It wouldn't be much, but I'd love you and care for you. Why I'd work night and day just to make things easy for you. I love you. It all begins and ends with that."

Elsie stood for a moment as though this honest appeal had touched her. Then she turned sharply.

"O, what's the use," she cried, "Look at this place. See how we live. And you—you want me to go on like this? No!"

Harvey stared at her stupidly.

"Don't stare at me like that," said the girl annoyed.

"I am wondering what has changed you so," said Harvey apologetically.

"Nothing, I tell you."

"Yes, there is something, or somebody."

"Now Harvey, please don't begin—" Elsie paused. Her glance left Harvey's face. A young man in a brown tweed suit and carrying a light walking stick in his gloved hand was coming toward the gate.

"Hello," he said easily, addressing Elsie and ignoring Spencer, "anybody at home?"

Elsie turned toward him with impulsive friendliness, then remembering her other suitor paused and tried to assume a manner of unconcern.

"Of course, there's someone at home," she said, "can't you see there is?"

"Can't be sure that such loveliness is real," said the new-comer gallantly.

"You're talking Chicagoese," said the girl, not, however, displeased.

"Simple fact, believe me," was the assured response.

Elsie saw that Harvey was eyeing the stranger with hostility. "Do you know Mr. Spencer, Mr. Druce?"

"Everybody in Millville knows Mr. Spencer," replied Martin Druce, putting out his hand. "He's a town institution."

"Thank you," said Harvey, mollified by what he thought a sincere compliment and shaking hands.

"Institution!" laughed Elsie.

Harvey stopped and withdrew the hand. It dawned on him that there was a secret understanding between Druce and the girl.

"Now hold on," he asked. "Just what do you mean by that word 'institution?'"

"Why you're one of the landmarks here," explained Druce, "the same as the bank or the opera house." He brushed the lapel of Harvey's coat with his gloved hand and straightened his collar. Then he soberly removed Harvey's straw hat, fingered it into grotesque lines and replaced it on his head. He stepped back to observe the effect, adding satirically: "I'll bet you won't stay long in this jay town."

"You're dead right there," boasted Harvey. "Millville is all right and a rising place but—"

"I knew it," said Druce gravely. "You'll be coming up to Chicago to show Marshall Field how to run his store."

"Well, I may—" began Harvey proudly.

"Oh!" Elsie's voice was pained. "Don't do that, Mr. Druce!" Then she turned to Spencer. "Why do you let him make a joke of you?"

"Who? Me?" Harvey looked at her in astonishment. He turned to Druce savagely. "Say," he demanded, "are you trying to kid me?"

"Not on your life," was the reply. "I knew better than to try to kid a wise young man like you. What I'm trying to say is that you're too big for this town. Say, what's your ambition?"

"Oh, I've got one, Mr. Druce. I'm going to be a detective."

"Well, there's lots of room for a real one in Chicago," said Druce, suppressing a contemptuous smile.

"I may go there some day."

"Come along," said Druce, "the more the merrier."

"Say, Mr. Druce," asked Harvey, now completely taken in by the ingratiating stranger, "what's your business?"

"Mine, why—" The man moved toward Elsie as he spoke, gazing at her steadily.

"Yes, you've got one, haven't you?" persisted Harvey.

Druce seemed confused for a moment. Then his face broke into a genial smile. Both Elsie and Spencer were watching him curiously.

"Sure, I've got a business. It's a mighty profitable one, too. I'm a dealer in live stock."

"Oh, cattle?" said Harvey.

"You got me," was the casual response, "just cattle."

CHAPTER V

A SERPENT WHISPERS AND A WOMAN LISTENS

The word cattle seemed to arouse the roan colt to his own existence. He whinnied ingratiatingly and tugged at his hitching strap. Whether or not his master had forgotten, he knew it was supper time. Harvey heard him.

"Well," he said to Druce, backing away towards the gate. "I've got to be going. Drop into the store some time. I'll give you a cigar."

"Thanks," laughed Druce. Then under his breath he added, "Like blazes I will." He turned back to Elsie. "Is that the Rube," he demanded, "who wants to marry you?"

"Yes," defended Elsie hotly, "and he's all right, too. I don't think it was nice of you to make fun of him as you did."

"Now, now," said Druce soothingly. "Don't be angry with me. I was just playing around." He paused and looked warily at the house. "Everything all right, eh?"

"Yes, I guess so," replied Elsie, with an anxious look in the same direction. "Harvey frightened me when I first got home. For a moment I thought he knew that I had been out with you."

"Well, what if he did? There's no harm in going for a ride with me, is there?"

"No-o," Elsie shook her head doubtfully. "But I don't feel just right about it."

"And that grocery fellow didn't know after all, eh?"

"I think not. At least he said nothing."

Druce shrugged his shoulders derisively.

"I think not. At least he said nothing." he couldn't detect a hair in the butter. I'm not worried about him. How is it with your own folks? Your mother doesn't know?"

"No," replied Elsie, uneasy again. "Anyway, mother wouldn't matter so much, but dad—" She covered her face with her hands.

"Never mind," said Druce tenderly, drawing her toward him and caressing her. "We had some ride, didn't we?"

"Grand," replied Elsie, brightened by the recollection.

"I told you it would be all right if I hired the car and picked you up around the corner from the mill. Say—" The man lowered his tone. "Gee, you're prettier than ever today, Elsie!"

Something in his manner caused the girl to recoil. The shrinking movement did not escape Druce.

"What's the matter, girlie?" he inquired. "Do you know that

in all the weeks I have been coming down here from Chicago to see you, you haven't even kissed me?"

"Please," pleaded the girl, pushing him away. She scarcely understood her mood. She only knew she did not want Druce to touch her.

"What's the matter?" repeated Druce, following close behind her.

"I—I don't know," faltered the girl, "I feel wicked somehow."

"Why?" He led her to a bench and sat down beside her. "Haven't I always treated you like a lady?"

"Yes, Martin, you've been good to me—but—I feel wicked."

Druce laughed. "Nonsense, girlie," he said, "you couldn't be wicked if you tried. Do you know what you ought to do?"

"What?" she asked.

"Turn your back on this town where nothing ever happens and come to little old Chicago, the live village by the lake."

"Chicago! What could I do there?"

"Make more money in a month than you can earn here in a year."

"But how?"

"You can sing," said Druce appraisingly. "You're there forty ways when it comes to looks. Why they'd pay you a hundred dollars a week to sing in the cabarets."

"Cabarets?" The girl's interest was aroused. "What's a cabaret?"

"A cabaret," said Druce, "is a restaurant where ladies and gentlemen dine. A fine great hall, polished floors, rugs, palms, a lot of little tables, colored lights, flowers, silver, cut glass, perfumes, a grand orchestra—get that in your mind—and then the orchestra strikes up and you come down the aisle, right through the crowd and sing to them."

"Oh, I'd love to do that," said the girl.

"Why not try it?"

"I—I wouldn't know how to begin."

"I'll show you how."

"Tell me, tell me how, quick."

"Dead easy," Druce explained smoothly. "I'm going back to Chicago on the evening train tonight. Now there's no use having trouble with your folks. They wouldn't understand. You tell them you are going over to one of the neighbors', anything you can think of. That train slows down at the junction, right across the field there—you can always hear it whistle. I'll be aboard the last car and I'll take you to Chicago with me. Then when we get there we—"

He broke off abruptly for Elsie started up from the bench and moved slowly away.

"What's the matter, girlie?" asked Druce.

"I—I don't know," the girl answered. "There isn't anyone here but just us, is there?"

"No," replied Druce, watching the girl closely, "why?"

"Because," she half whispered, "it seemed to me just then that someone touched me on the arm and said, 'Don't go!'"

Druce started. He looked carefully around. Then he laughed.

"You're hearing things tonight, Elsie," he said. "There's no one here but just you and me." He took her by the hand and was drawing her down to the bench when suddenly the front door of the cottage opened and Mrs. Welcome appeared.

"Elsie," she called. She stood framed in the lighted doorway, her eyes shaded with her hand. Like a shadow Druce faded from his seat beside the girl and dodged behind a tree out of sight, but in hearing.

"Is that you, Elsie?" asked the mother. "I thought I heard voices. Was Harvey here?"

"Yes," replied the girl in confusion, "he has just gone."

"You didn't see anything of your father, did you?"

Elsie shook her head. "You—you don't suppose dad's drinking again?" the girl asked anxiously.

"I suppose so," replied the mother wearily. "He hasn't been here all day."

"Oh, mother," the girl wailed. "What shall we do?" She sank down on the seat.

Her mother took her in her arms. "Don't cry," she said. "Come in and help me get supper."

"I'm waiting for Patience," replied the girl. "I'll be in the house in a moment. You go ahead with the work. When Patience comes we'll both help you."

Mrs. Welcome walked back into the cottage. As the door closed behind her Druce reappeared. He had not missed a word of the conversation between Elsie and her mother; as he now approached he outlined in his mind an immediate plan of attack.

"Elsie," he said softly. The girl started.

"I thought you had gone," she said. "No, don't touch me. I'm in trouble. My father—" she covered her face with her hands.

"Yes, I know," said Druce. "I heard it all. Why do you stay here? Why do you—"

"It isn't that," retorted the girl, too proud to accept sympathy. "You made me lie to my mother. That is the first time I ever deceived my mother."

"Don't cry," said Druce. He drew her to the bench. "Come," he went on, "be sensible. Dry those tears. Come with me to Chicago."

"How do you know I could get a chance to sing in that place you told me of?" she demanded, open to argument.

Druce pressed his advantage. "Why," he said, "I'm interested in one myself. I think I could arrange to place you."

"Martin," said Elsie, "you said you were in the live stock business."

Druce hesitated a moment, toying with his cane. "I am," he

said slowly. "This cabaret—er—is a little speculation on the side. Come now, say you'll be at the train at eight o'clock."

The girl considered long.

"Think," said Druce, "with one hundred dollars a week you will be able to take your mother out of this hole. Why, you'll be independent! You owe it to your family not to let this opportunity escape you."

"I'll go," said Elsie.

"Good! Good for you, I mean," said Druce.

"On one condition," the girl went on.

"What do you mean?"

Elsie got up from her seat embarrassed. "It all depends," she said.

"On what?" demanded Druce.

"On you, Martin."

"Me?" Druce laughed uneasily.

"Yes," said the girl walking close to him and looking him in the face. "There is only one way I can go to Chicago with you."

"How's that, girlie?" was Druce's astonished question.

Elsie held up her left hand timidly. "With a plain gold ring on that finger, Martin," she said. She was now blushing furiously. She knew that she had virtually proposed to Druce. He laughed and something in his laugh jarred her.

"Oh, marriage," he said.

"You know that Martin, don't you? I couldn't go to Chicago with you any other way."

Druce took off his hat. "Elsie," he said, "you're as good as gold. I honor you for your scruples."

He paused to think for a moment. "I'll tell you," he said. "You come along with me and I'll marry you as soon as we reach Chicago. Meanwhile I'll telegraph ahead and arrange to have you taken care of by my old aunt. You'll be as safe with her as if you were in your own home."

"You promise to marry me?"

"Sure I do, girlie." He broke off blusteringly. "What do you take me for? Do you think I'd lure you to Chicago and then leave you?"

"Martin," said Elsie gravely, "a girl must protect herself."

"You'll go, honey?" Druce persisted.

"I can't tell," replied the girl desperately, anxious to promise and yet afraid.

"You'll go," said Druce positively, "at eight o'clock—"

A cool voice broke in on his sentence. Druce started like a man suddenly drenched with cold water.

"What's that is going to happen at eight o'clock, Mr. Druce?"

The speaker was Patience Welcome.

CHAPTER VI

A ROMANCE DAWNS—AND A TRAGEDY

Patience Welcome shared all the prejudices of her employer, John Price, against "city chaps." Her observation of those who had presented themselves in Millville had not raised her estimate of them. As a class she found them overdressed and underbred. They came into her small town obsessed with the notion of their superiority. Patience had been at some pains in a quiet way to puncture the pretensions of as many as came within scope of her sarcasm. She was not, like many girls of Millville, so much overwhelmed by the glamour of Chicago that she believed every being from that metropolis must be of a superior breed. She had penetration enough to estimate them at their true value. In her frankness, she made no effort to conceal her sentiments toward them.

But recently there had come into her acquaintance a product of Chicago whom she could not fit into Mr. Price's city chap category. This was Harry Boland.

Young Boland, the son of Chicago's "electrical king," was himself president of his father's Lake City Electrical Company. He was good looking, quiet, competent and totally lacking in the bumptiousness that Patience found so offensive in other Chicago youths. Toward him Patience had been compelled to modify her usual attitude of open aversion to mere cold reserve. She did not quite comprehend him and until conviction of his merits came she was determined to occupy the safe ground of suspicion.

Patience and Harry Boland had first met on a basis that could scarcely have been more formal. The young man, early in his business career, had been his father's collector. Part of his duties had consisted of collecting the rents of a large number of workmen's cottages which the elder Boland owned at Millville. The Welcomes occupied one of these cottages. As Tom Welcome not infrequently was unable to pay the rent when it was due, Boland had had numerous opportunities for seeing Patience, who was treasurer of the Welcome household.

Her attitude toward him had at first amused, then annoyed and finally interested him. When he began to understand what was back of her coldness a respect, such as he had felt for no other girl, developed in him. The more she held him off the more eager he became for a better acquaintance. This desire was fed by her repulses. Long ago he had made up his mind that he loved her. Now, in spite of the social chasm that yawned between them, he was determined to win her. His intentions toward her were honor itself. He was determined to marry her.

When Harvey Spencer drove off, after having introduced Patience to Grogan, the girl started toward her home. She had gone only a short distance when a quick step behind her appraised her that she was followed. A moment later Harry Boland appeared at her side, hat in hand.

"How do you do, Miss Welcome?"

"I'm very well, thank you," replied Patience, primly.

"Beautiful day, isn't it?" demanded Harry inanely.

"Yes," agreed Patience, "I love the spring and even Millville is beautiful now."

"I think it the most beautiful place in the world," declared Harry enthusiastically.

Patience looked at him in surprise, then colored and laughed. "Do you?" she said with the accent on the first word.

"I hope," said Harry, "that you don't mind if I smoke."

"Not at all."

There was an awkward silence.

"Patience," Harry used the girl's name for the first time with deliberation, "why don't you speak to me?"

Patience did not resent the familiarity. "I am thinking," she replied.

"You act as though you do not like me. What have I done?"

"It's not that," replied Patience shortly.

"Then you are trying to avoid me."

"I am."

"Why?"

"Don't you know?" She turned and looked at him squarely. She was determined to dispose of his attentions then and there.

"I'm not good at riddles."

"Think a moment, then. You are Harry Boland, only son of the richest and most powerful man in Chicago. I am Patience Welcome, daughter of a broken inventor, tenant in a cottage which you own, where I cannot pay the rent. Can there be anything in common between us?"

Harry ignored the question. "You have forgotten one fact," he said. There was determination in his voice. "Or don't you know it?"

"What is that?" asked Patience over her shoulder, for she had turned from him.

"That Harry Boland is in love with Patience Welcome."

"What an absurdity!"

"You don't believe me?"

"How can you talk like that to me?" said the girl, now agitated. "Look at me. You know we are in arrears for rent."

"Don't worry about that."

She turned on him defiantly and looked into his eyes. Then her glance fell under his more burning one. She flushed and turned away.

"I suppose," she said, huskily with humiliation, "that you have paid the rent yourself." She was almost in tears.

"Now don't take it like that," pleaded Harry. "No one but you and me will ever know. And if you will let me I will take you away from all this."

Patience raised her head. She had recovered her composure.

"All men come to that finally," she said coldly. "Even in my slight experience I have learned the phrase almost by heart. All men say that. They offer—"

"Just a moment." Harry put out his hand emphatically. "Wait! All the men in your slight experience may have said it, but all have not meant it. I mean that if I take you away from all this I shall take you as Mrs. Harry Boland—as my wife."

"Harry!" His name was wrenched from the girl's very heart by her surprise.

"Do you believe that I love you now?" demanded Boland.

"Yes. I didn't know, I didn't understand. I have wronged you ever since I have known you. Forgive me. But your father?"

"Let me call your attention to the fact," said Harry, planting himself firmly before her, "that I am many years past the age of seven—and can choose a wife for myself."

"But your father?" insisted Patience.

"Oh, he may rage and fume," retorted Harry, "but I have a standing of my own. I am president of the Lake City Electric Company that controls dad's patent light."

"My father was interested in electricity, too—before—"

But Harry interrupted her. "Never mind our fathers," he said. "We are the chief characters in this romance, you know."

They had reached the path leading to the Welcome cottage.

Patience, eager to end the interview which had thrown her into a state of consternation, such as she had never experienced before, seized the present opportunity.

"Harry," she said, "please go. We are expecting father home and—I'm afraid—it won't be pleasant."

"You haven't answered me. I'm off to Chicago tomorrow."

"Tomorrow!" Patience caught her breath quickly.

"Yes, in my new car. I'm going to drive back. I've overstayed my time and there are business calls which I simply cannot ignore. I'll not insist on an answer tonight, but will you write me?"

The girl put out her hand which Harry grasped. Her lips quivered and she breathed, "Yes."

He lifted the hand to his lips, but the girl drew it from him, whispered "goodby" and darted away. He stood watching her until she disappeared. Patience hurrying toward the cottage was roused from her tumult of emotion by the sound of voices. Once she heard the words "eight o'clock," without recognizing the speaker. When they were spoken again she knew the voice as that of Martin Druce. She disliked Druce. The thought of his being alone with Elsie chilled her.

She came toward him swiftly but in silence. Her question: "What did you say was going to happen at eight o'clock, Mr. Druce?" was a complete surprise.

"Eh—why—" stammered Druce, off his guard.

"Why Patience, how late you are," interrupted Elsie to conceal Druce's confusion.

"Just a little, dear," replied Patience, now confused herself. "I have been busy at the store." Then she turned to Druce again. "What is it about eight o'clock—is it something concerning Elsie?" she persisted.

"O, I was just saying that I had to meet a man at the hotel at eight," returned Druce, full of assurance again.

"Ah!" said Patience, "well, you'll catch him all right—if you start now."

Druce laughed. "Here's your hat—what's your hurry, eh?"

"Patience, how can you?" demanded Elsie.

"I didn't mean to be rude," retorted Patience serenely, "only I wouldn't have him miss that man."

"Oh, I can take a hint." Druce started for the gate. As he reached it he turned back to the two girls and added:

"I sure hope that man keeps his appointment to meet me at eight o'clock."

CHAPTER VII

HARRY BOLAND HEARS FROM HIS FATHER

Harry Boland strode away from his interview with Patience deeply occupied with tumultuous reflections, not seeing the beauties of Millville which, but a short time before, he had been enthusiastically celebrating. He was, in fact, a young man walking in a dream. Every word the girl had uttered, every inflection of her voice, the involuntary confession of affection won from her by his own no less sudden avowal of love, projected themselves against his excited mind with all the vividness of kinetoscope pictures. He was very happy with these reflections that come to the youth in love when a familiar voice suddenly recalled him to mundane things.

"Hello, there Harry," said the voice.

It was Grogan's.

"Hello," replied Harry, roused but not displeased to meet his father's intimate political adviser in this part of the world, "what are you doing in this part of Illinois?"

"I'm on my way home," replied Grogan, laconically.

"Ah, yes, Dad wrote me. You went to Kansas City, didn't you?"

"I did. Your father caught me on the wire at St. Louis."

"What did the governor want?"

"Nothing much. He told me you were here and suggested that I meet you. He thought it would be pleasant for us both to have company home."

It dawned on Harry that perhaps his father had not been quite disinterested in this.

"You're a good politician, Mike," he said shortly.

"Is that a compliment now, or a slander against my character?" Grogan demanded, smiling.

"Neither," replied Harry. "It's a fact."

"And why, might I ask, have you recalled it at this particular moment?"

"Because your conversation in this particular instance seemed to me to be that of a person who was concealing something. Politician's talk, Grogan, is specious, but notable for its reticence."

"Well, Harry," returned Grogan, "your own line of talk is not particularly illuminating, either."

"What do you mean, Mike?"

"Well, here I am, an old friend of your father's, mixed up with him in half a dozen deals. I've known you ever since you sat in a high chair and spooned gruel from a bowl. I come on you in this out of the way corner and you say never a word of why you're here, or what you're doing. I think

Clam is your middle name."

"Why," replied Harry, "I came down to Millville to collect some rents."

"Only rents?" queried Grogan pointedly.

"What the devil do you mean?"

"Youngsters of your age sometimes amuse themselves collecting—shirtwaists."

"Stop that, Grogan," retorted Harry angrily.

"Stop what, me boy?"

"I don't like that sort of insinuation."

"Ho," said Grogan, "angry, eh? Then it's as I thought. There's always fire in the heart when a young man flares up about a girl."

"Look here, Grogan—"

"Easy, boy," interrupted the older man. "I'm your friend and I don't want to see you get into trouble—with your father, I mean."

"Did he send you to spy on me?" demanded Harry hotly.

"Not at all," returned Grogan suavely, "only he's worried."

"Worried, what the devil about?"

Grogan did not reply.

"I know I've overstayed my time," Harry went on, "but some of these people have been difficult. I couldn't throw them into the street when they promised to pay and—"

"I know, I know," put in Grogan. "It's not about you. Your father's worried about business. One of these crazy reform waves has started in Chicago. A vice investigating committee is raising ructions."

"What do you mean by a reform wave? What can a vice investigating committee have to do with my father?"

"Well, you see," Grogan was picking his words carefully, "your father has large interests. An investigation of that sort unsettles business."

"What started the reform wave?"

"A girl."

"A what?"

"I said a girl," replied Grogan evenly.

Harry laughed.

"Yes," said Grogan, "they all laughed at her at first, just as you are doing now. But the joke is beginning to lose its point."

"Who is she?"

"Her name," returned Grogan, "is Mary Randall."

"Mary Randall," repeated Harry. The words meant nothing to him. "Who is she?"

"I don't know," replied Grogan. "I've never met the lady. That's the mystery of her and she's keeping it well. She belongs to the Randalls of Chicago—society folk—that's all I know. But she isn't one of these Michigan boulevard tea party reformers. They just talk. She goes out and delivers the goods. She's a fighter."

Harry laughed again. "This is good," he said. "An unknown girl, a society bud, working single handed stirs up Chicago until she gets all of you alleged smart politicians worrying. Grogan, I'm going to write a comedy about that."

"Are you now?" said Grogan. "Well, I don't approve of your idea. It's not funny. The other night they raided the Baker Club and when they came into court they had evidence enough to hang them all. This Randall girl had worked in the club for a month as a waitress and she KNEW."

"Still, Mike, that shouldn't affect father."

"Not directly—no," replied Grogan, again picking his words with care, "but it gives the whole city an unsteady feeling. People won't invest their money. If I were in your place, my boy, I'd go home."

"I'm off tomorrow in my new car. Better come with me."

"Make it tonight and I will," replied Grogan.

"You're on," agreed Harry. "We'll go tonight." He surveyed the sky. "It's going to storm," he said; "but even if it does, unless there's a flood the roads will be good. We'll go tonight."

CHAPTER VIII

THE DEATH OF TOM WELCOME

Both Harry Boland and Grogan fell silent after having reached their agreement to return to Chicago immediately. To a degree both men regretted the decision.

Grogan had accomplished the purpose for which the elder Boland had despatched him to Millville—that of disentangling Harry from his romance—but what he had seen of Patience Welcome had led him to dislike his task.

Harry had no sooner promised to drive back to Chicago in the night than he was assailed with yearning to see the girl again. Each occupied himself with his own thoughts. Dusk descended on the village. They had reached the corner of the street that led to their hotel when they were arrested by a maudlin voice.

"I'm all right, I tell you, Harve."

Two men came out from beneath the shadow of the trees and could be seen dimly under the sickly gleam of a street light. One leaned heavily against the other.

"Sure, you're all right," replied the drunken man's companion

62   Virginia Brooks

in a voice both recognized as that of Harvey Spencer. "I'm just going to see you as far as your house." He spoke in the voice people use in humoring drunken men and children.

"I hain't drunk, Harve," insisted Harvey's companion.

"Of course, you ain't," replied Harvey, "come on."

"I'm just overcome with the heat. I—"

The reeling man broke off suddenly. He saw Harry and Grogan.

"Who the devil are you?" he demanded truculently.

"My name is Harry Boland," replied the young man.

"Oh, the son of John Boland, eh?" jeered the drunken man. "Son of John Boland, 'lectric light king. John Boland's son, eh?"

"Yes," replied Harry sharply, "what of it?"

"Nothing I can prove," retorted Welcome, grimly, "only— give my regards to your father. Just tell him Tom Welcome sends his regards. He'll know." He began to whimper softly. "Poor old Tom Welcome, who might have been riding in his carriage this day." He stopped whining abruptly and snarled at the young man: "If there was any justice on God's earth—"

Welcome lurched forward. Harry grasped his wrist and peered into his bloated face.

"What do you mean by that?" he demanded.

Grogan interrupted a good deal agitated. "He doesn't mean

anything," he said, "he's just drunk. Come, boy, let's get out of here."

"I want to know—" persisted Harry, but he dropped Welcome's arm.

"Don't be a fool," commanded Grogan, "can't you see the man's drunk? Come on."

"But I tell you I want to know—"

"Oh, you don't know anything!"

Harry was about to retort angrily when Grogan seized his wrist with an iron grip and swung him around the corner. Half dragging the young man along with him he got him to the hotel. There Grogan succeeded in convincing him of the folly of engaging in a street argument with a dipsomaniac he did not know.

Meanwhile Harvey and Welcome continued their slow and stumbling journey to the Welcome cottage. Welcome, after his interview with Harry Boland was in a savage mood. A debauch of two days had left him virtually a mad man. It required all of Harvey's diplomacy to get him into his house quietly.

The lights were burning in the living room when they arrived. Harvey convoyed his swaying companion to the back of the house, opened the door quietly and pushed him in. Mrs. Welcome and the two girls were in the living room, but the wind was sighing without and they heard nothing. A storm had come up with the setting of the sun and occasional flashes of lightning lighted the darkened room where Welcome found himself while the thunder deadened the sound of his stumbling feet. He made his way through the kitchen to a bedroom and sank down exhausted on a bed.

But Tom Welcome could not sleep. Every nerve in his body jangled. The interview with young Boland, for reasons which will be apparent to the reader later, had aroused in him a smouldering anger. He tossed restlessly on his couch.

While he lay there he heard some one knocking at the front door. All of his perceptions had grown abnormally keen. He heard a boy's voice and recognized it as that of a neighbor's son.

"It's me, Jimmie," said the boy. "Pa sent me over with Elsie's veil. She dropped it while she was out in the auto this afternoon."

He heard the door close and then the accusing voice of his wife demanding:

"Elsie, who have you been out with, automobiling?"

"I was out this afternoon with Martin Druce," replied the girl defiantly.

"Then," went on the mother, conscious that a crisis of some sort between her and her daughter was approaching, "you were talking to him this evening and not to Harvey Spencer? You told me a falsehood?"

"What if I did?" Elsie's tone was low and stubborn.

Mrs. Welcome began to sob.

"Mother, mother," pleaded Patience, "Elsie didn't mean—"

"I did mean it," flared back Elsie. "I did mean it! Why

shouldn't I go autoing when I have the chance? Isn't life in Millville hard enough without—" She paused overcome by a wave of passion. "I'm tired of Millville," she exclaimed, "I'm tired of the factory. I'm tired of living here as we do in this miserable, tumble-down place we call home. I'm tired of working like a slave, while a drunken father—"

The words had scarcely left the girl's lips when Tom Welcome, red-eyed, dishevelled, swaying, appeared in the doorway behind her. His face was lit with demoniac passion. He rushed at the girl and she screamed in terror. With a vicious lunge he struck her down and then, seizing her by the hair, dragged her into the bedroom where, amid her cries, he rained blow after blow upon her.

Harvey Spencer, just passing through the gate, heard the first scream. He rushed back into the house as Welcome, finished for the moment with Elsie, had returned to the cottage living room and was approaching his wife menacingly. He seized the raging man by the collar and hurled him into a corner.

"Stay there," he said, "or I'll brain you."

Welcome stood for a moment glaring at the intruder. He attempted to speak, but foam flecked his lips and seemed to choke his voice. His eyes acquired a fixed and unearthly stare. He raised his fist as though to strike and then plunged headlong to the floor.

Patience was the first to reach her father's side. A vivid flash of lightning followed by a terrific detonation of thunder rocked the cottage.

"He's dying," screamed Patience.

Mrs. Welcome, forgetting past injuries, sprang to her

husband's side.

"Tom," she wailed, "speak to me. Tom—Tom, I'm your wife—"

The dying man tried to sit up. His mania had passed. He patted his wife's shoulder feebly and smiled. A great weakness had come into his face. "Forgive me," he said, "I didn't know—I didn't know what I was doing. It was the drink. I am going. Call Elsie!"

Patience sprang toward the bedroom, but it was empty. The open doors through the kitchen showed how she had fled. As she searched frantically for her sister, the little clock on the mantel slowly struck the hour of eight.

"She's gone," cried Patience. A premonition of the tragedy of Elsie's flight flashed upon her mind. "Oh," she cried, "my little lost sister! My little lost sister!"

"Gone," cried Harvey. "Gone where?" He opened the door. The rain was falling pitilessly. "Not out into this storm. Someone must find her." He rushed out into the darkness.

"Gone!" echoed Tom Welcome. His voice was hollow as a knell. The drink-racked body stiffened in a spasm and then dropped limply into his weeping wife's arms. "Gone!" he gasped.

Tom Welcome was dead.

Another flash of lightning and a roar of thunder. The two women strove to revive the corpse. At last the dreadful realization came to them that Tom Welcome would never speak again. The wind smote the cottage and the light in the single lamp in the room fluttered as though in mortal terror.

The skies were shattered with a final climactic crash of thunder. The mother and daughter, alone in that chamber of death, clung to each other silently feeling themselves isolated from all mankind, with even the elements storming against them.

While they waited, blanched and terror-stricken, for the last reverberations of the thunder, the whistle of the Fast Express, bound from Millville to the great city, rose wildly on the air, like the scream of an exultant demon, and died away in a series of weird and mocking echoes into the night.

CHAPTER IX

IN WHICH SOME OF CHICAGO'S BEST PEOPLE ESSAY A TASK TOO BIG FOR THEM

Lucas Randall inserted his key into the door and let himself into his Michigan boulevard residence. The butler, busy in one of the reception rooms, looked up merely to nod a welcome as he entered. Mr. Randall turned to the mirror in the hallway. He saw the reflection of a man sixty years of age, gray but well preserved, intelligent but not forceful.

As he turned from the glass he saw his wife descending the broad stairs. She was small and fragile. In her youth she had had a delicate pink and gold beauty. The years had worn away the pink and the gold but had left a spirituality that seemed even finer.

"I'm glad you're home early, Luke dear," he heard her saying. Then noticing his air of abstraction she added: "Did you forget after all, Luke?"

"Forget," he repeated blankly, "forget what, Lucy?"

"Oh you man!" replied his wife as if man were a word of reproach. "The church committee is to be here this afternoon to formulate its report on vice conditions."

"Oh, that!" Mr. Randall chuckled. "Yes, I had forgotten, but anyhow I made it, you see. How's Mary?"

"Very well—" Mrs. Randall broke off suddenly. There was a troubled look in her eyes. Then she added lightly almost to herself: "What a queer child!"

"Queer?"

"Yes, Luke, queer," returned Mrs. Randall. Again that troubled look. "Luke, dear, I want to make a confession. I don't understand Mary. After your brother Henry died, when we insisted that Mary come and live with us, it seemed wicked to leave her in that great house alone—and we have no children. Now, there are times I am almost sorry we did it. It isn't that I want to criticise Mary"—noticing her husband's look of surprise—"I know she loves us both and yet—well, I have the feeling that we don't really know her. The intimacy I had longed for hasn't developed. She seems to live a part of her time in another world than ours." She broke off again, laughing nervously. "Do you know," she said, "I sometimes have the feeling that Mary lives a sort of double life—nothing evil, you know—but uncanny. She's not unkind nor lacking in affection for either of us, but often when we are together it seems to me that her mind is miles away."

"Queer, eh?" said Mr. Randall, sympathetically. "Well, her father was like that."

"It's not strange if she is like her father," charged Mrs. Randall. "He brought her up like a boy. After her mother died she was more like a chum to him than a daughter."

Lucas Randall became meditative.

"The church work, now," he asked, "does she seem interested?"

"At first I think she was. I took her on some of my regular poor people calls. She seemed interested—too interested. Why, one day I lost her in a tenement on Kosciusko street. I had to come home without her, half wild with anxiety. She rushed in an hour later and when I questioned her as to where she had been she replied that she had found a poor Scotch family and had been so interested that she had forgotten me. 'Forgotten'—that's the very word she used. She said she had been 'seeking the causes of poverty.' I told her poverty came from people being poor, but that did not seem to satisfy her. She asked me why they were poor. I answered that often it was because they were shiftless. 'Not always,' she replied, 'these Scotch people, aunt, dear, were strangely like you and me.' She spoke as if I were the one who did not understand."

"And since then?"

"Well, she has seemed to prefer going alone." Mrs. Randall paused on the verge of a new confession. "Luke, dear," she went on hurriedly, "Mary goes into sections of the city you have warned me not to visit!"

"Not the Levee?"

"Just that."

"Good Lord," ejaculated Mr. Randall, "surely she doesn't go alone?"

"Yes, except for her maid."

"That girl she took from the Refuge?"

"Anna."

"Where is Mary now?"

"In her room."

"She'll come down to the committee meeting, I suppose?"

"I asked her and she replied that of course she would come."

"Has she been out today, Lucy?"

"Nearly all day."

"Calls, I suppose."

"No, she's been attending the hearings of the vice commission."

"In God's name, why?" Mr. Randall was really disturbed.

"I asked her that very question. She replied that the proceedings interested her."

"Heavens!" Mr. Randall paced the room. "'Interested' her! A girl with an income she can't possibly spend, a girl who might have anything, do anything, go anywhere, marry any man—"

He broke off suddenly. "Lucy," he demanded, "is there any man Mary might care for? That good looking young curate, for instance?"

Mrs. Randall shook her head emphatically. "No, Luke," she said. "If you were to ask me to name the two things Mary never gives a thought to I'd say men and matrimony. And that's another thing about her I cannot fathom."

Further confidences were cut short by the entrance of the butler announcing the Rev. Thomas Brattle, a clergyman of sixty with an old fashioned flowing white beard, small white hands and shiny gold-bowed spectacles, and Marvin Lattimer, a business man with a turn for religious activities. Desultory conversation followed broken by the entrance of Mrs. Sumnet-Ives, a well preserved woman of forty and a social power, and Miss Emma Laforth, slender, dark, intelligent looking and gifted with a political acumen that had given her an unassailable position in women's club circles. They were escorted by Grove Evans, plump, wealthy, well born, mildly interested in reform because reform was the proper thing, and Wyat Carp, a lawyer with literary tendencies.

Greetings and small talk; then Lucas Randall led the way to the library. There the Rev. Mr. Brattle, clearing his throat in an official manner, established himself before a priceless seventeenth century table of carved mahogany.

"The meeting will come to order," he announced.

A circle of chairs had been drawn up before the table. The committee members occupied them with a subdued rustle of garments. The Rev. Mr. Brattle watched the circle benignly, waiting for a moment of total silence. When he spoke his voice was smooth, finely modulated, pitched in the right key. His manner, in fact, was perfect. Indeed, in the spacious luxury of Lucas Randall's fine library no one could have appeared to better advantage.

"Dear friends," he said, beaming about him, "we are gathered here, as you know, to formulate the report of our investigation into vice conditions. You have labored long and faithfully. Now the time has come to put forth the fruit of your labors in a form at once concrete and illuminating."

He paused, then continued:

"The problem we are approaching is world-old. Mankind has struggled with it intermittently since civilization began. Apparently we have made no progress. The twentieth century, in fact, with its terrific congestion in cities, its vast consumption of nervous energy and its universal comercialism, has complicated our problem. But with these new complications have come new means for warring against the evil. Intelligence on the subject is more general. Fine minds everywhere are addressing themselves to the riddle. Thus it seems that humanity is at last coming to grips with the traffic in women. Who knows but that out of this little gathering may not be evolved some theory which, injected into the circulation of modern life, shall immunize us against this social malady."

There was subdued applause.

"As my time has been somewhat occupied," the clergyman went on, "I have asked Mr. Carp to employ his well known literary gift in formulating our report. Let me add that I have read our brother's resume of our investigations and endorse it fully as to the facts found."

Meanwhile Wyat Carp, with his best poet's air, had arisen and bowed to the little circle. He laid a terrifying number of manuscript sheets on the table and polished his glasses with his silk handkerchief. His was the subdued manner of a surgeon about to perform an operation and, it must be confessed, his audience felt some of the sensations of the patient.

Virginia Brooks

"My friends," began Wyat Carp, "in putting before you what I trust you may see fit to adopt as our united report I am naturally moved by a feeling of delicacy—"

He paused, for directly behind the little circle of hearers the heavy curtains had been pushed aside, and a girl stood framed there against the dull red of the draperies. She was rather above medium height, with a figure rounded by exercise, a face oval and lighted by deep blue eyes underneath masses of burnished, coppery hair. Her personality seemed to fill the room. She breathed wholesomeness, vigor, sincerity and purpose.

As Lucas Randall half started from his chair the girl put out her hand and checked him.

"No, Uncle Luke," she said, "don't disturb yourself. I've been standing just outside the door for several minutes waiting for a moment to slip in quietly."

She bowed to them all, and seated herself near the window overlooking the boulevard.

"Just go on with the report, Mr. Carp," she said, "I assure you I am most eager to hear it."

Wyat Carp coughed gently and picked up his manuscript.

"Thank you, Miss Randall," he began gravely, "I—I—"

"You were saying that you were moved by a feeling of delicacy," prompted the girl.

"Thank you, Miss Randall." Mr. Carp bowed. "I—er—am experiencing a feeling of embarrassment because this is a meeting of both sexes and the subject is one which, only recently, has been discussed in mixed company. When one so young as yourself is present—"

"Oh," replied the girl, a shade of amusement in her voice, "please don't let my youth interfere with our deliberations. I assure you that, young as I may appear to be, I am quite familiar with the matter we have under consideration."

This remarkable declaration caused something of a real sensation. Mrs. Sumnet-Ives mentally put the speaker down as "a pert little chit." Grove Evans was amused, for he disliked Carp. Mrs. Randall catalogued it as another ebullition of Mary's queerness; even her uncle, despite an affection that accepted everything Mary did as right and proper, felt himself a little shocked. As for Miss Laforth, she favored Miss Randall with a long, inventorying inspection. Here, she reflected, might be a future political rival.

Mr. Carp began to read slowly with here and there a pause to enable his audience to catch a subtle turn of phrase or the flowing rhythm of his periods. He read while the light grew fainter and the fire glowed more brightly, read until Lucas Randall leaned across the table and switched on the light in the great brass lamp.

Mary Randall, deep in her easy chair beside the window and lulled by the soporific monotone of Mr. Carp's voice, saw the afternoon darken into dusk and the dusk deepen into night. Before her half-closed eyes the city, slowly but purposefully, began to throw off the habiliments of day and don the tinsel of evening. One by one, from far down the spacious avenue, the street lamps glowed into bulbs of color which the wet asphalt, like a winding black mirror, caught up and flung against the polished finishings of a swift and silent train of automobiles and the windows of the nearby mansions.

Virginia Brooks

And still Wyat Carp read on and on, skirting the outer circle of forbidden subjects, leading up to closed doors he made no attempt to open, expatiating voluminously on conditions that all the world knew, elucidating the obvious, ranging from one platitude to another—and avoiding the vital and concrete as though it were poisonous. And as Mr. Carp read Mary became oppressed with his total futility.

Mrs. Ives risked a hasty glance at her jeweled wrist watch.

"Doesn't the man know it's nearly time to dine?" she wondered.

Grove Evans, with a dinner engagement at the club and a place bespoken in a quiet poker game afterward, squirmed in his chair and cursed Wyat Carp silently. Finally, with a last rhetorical flourish, Mr. Carp quite suddenly ended. He sat down amid a murmur of applause.

"Wonderful," exclaimed Mrs. Ives. She was agreeably astonished that Mr. Carp should ever have finished.

"Very full, concise and to the point," was Miss Laforth's verdict.

"Great!" announced Grove Evans, really delighted, for he would be in time for dinner at the club after all.

The Rev. Thomas Brattle gazed about the circle with a bland smile. "I am glad," he said, "to have my judgment indorsed by such excellent critics."

Then, rapping gently on the table, he glanced about him. "A motion is in order before we adjourn, my friends," he stated, expectantly.

"I move Mr. Carp's report be adopted as it stands," said Marvin Lattimer breathlessly. He had waited patiently all afternoon to speak just those words. His business judgment, as applied to social affairs, had taught him the wisdom of getting into the record. He was only a recent confidant of this inner circle of All Souls and he aspired to remain where he was. Besides, it would be something to tell the socially ambitious Mrs. Lattimer when he got home. There was a second from Miss Laforth.

"You hear the motion," breathed the reverend chairman. "Those in favor will please say 'aye.'" As they all responded he beamed upon them. He turned with a deprecatory glance to Carp. "And as a matter of form, those contrary minded will please signify by saying 'no.'"

He waited a moment. Quite clearly and distinctly Mary Randall spoke:

"No!"

The tiny monosyllable seemed to echo and reecho through the high-ceiled room. There was a most embarrassing silence.

"Mary," faltered Mrs. Randall.

Mary came over and pressed her hand against her aunt's shoulder. "Believe me," she said, "I don't mean to wound you. You don't understand." Then turning to the Rev. Mr. Brattle, she went on: "But I must insist that my vote in the negative be recorded in the minutes of this meeting."

"May I inquire the cause of your—er—peculiar attitude?" asked the clergyman.

"Do you think that fair, Dr. Brattle?"

"Possibly not fair, but perhaps our curiosity is pardonable."
There was suppressed sarcasm in his retort.

"In your little speech of introduction, my dear doctor," said
the girl, "you advanced the suggestion that this meeting
might evolve some theory that would rid society of the social
evil. The great trouble with this report is that it is all theory. I
have no quarrel with the facts that Mr. Carp has given us,
except that they are old—'world old,' as I think you said.
Weeks have been spent on this investigation and yet there is
not one word—not a single word—that answers the appeal
going up in this city day after day from thousands of un-
fortunate women. We sit here, after weeks of investigation,
and listen to a homily. The time is past in Chicago for
homilies. The question is: What are we going to do about it?
Helpless thousands are asking us that question and we
answer it with a treatise full of 'world-old' truth and full of
'theory.' Mr. Carp speaks of the resorts on Dunkirk street
being 'questionable'—"

"They are questionable," defended Mr. Carp stoutly.

"Questionable, Mr. Carp," replied Mary, "is a gentle word.
These resorts are a shrieking infamy. They are markets in
which young girls are sold like cattle."

"How do you know that?" demanded Grove Evans, almost
rudely. He felt his club appointment slipping away from him
and the poker game owed him two hundred dollars.

Mary looked from her aunt to her uncle.

"I know," she replied, "because I have been there. I know
because I myself bought four girls there!"

The company gasped its surprise.

"I told them I was 'in the business' in Seattle," the speaker continued. "I told them I wanted to buy. I asked for four girls—four young girls. They sold me four for one hundred dollars each."

There was a silence for a long moment. It was broken by Marvin Lattimer.

"Impossible!" he exclaimed.

Mary looked at him sadly. "There is one fact more impossible than that, Mr. Lattimer," she said. "It is that men of the world like you—men who, above all others, should make it their business to know these things,—cry out 'Impossible!' when such a fact is exhibited before you in all its hideousness."

"You should have had the man who sold those girls arrested," blurted Grove Evans.

"I did," replied Mary quietly, "and *The Reporter*, in which you are a part owner, suppressed publication of the fact. I had the man arrested and Jim Edwards, the politician who holds the district in the hollow of his hand, prevented the case from going to trial. That man walks the streets of Chicago free and without bond."

The girl turned to Dr. Brattle again.

"Doctor," she said, "you are a clergyman. You are the shepherd of the flock. Are you, too, deaf to the appeal that goes up daily from the sinks of this city,—from hundreds of ruined girls? Do you, too, stand by while wolves rend the lambs? Do you deny the existence of the wolf?"

"We can only strive to educate these women, to teach them the error of their way," pleaded the shepherd.

"But, doctor, while you are educating one, the wolves are tearing down twenty. They 'educate,' too, and their facilities are better than yours."

The girl stopped breathlessly and, stooping swiftly, kissed her aunt. There were tears in her eyes.

"Don't worry about me," she said.

Then suddenly she crossed the room and threw open the door. The maid, Anna, stood there with a satchel at her feet and Mary's cloak upon her arm. Mary picked up the satchel and turned toward the street door.

"The time for theory alone is over," she said, addressing the company. "Someone has got to go into action against the wolves."

The door swung behind her and she stepped out into the boulevard.

CHAPTER X

THE ADVENTURES OF A NEWSPAPER STORY

Great cities thrive on sensations. The yellow journal with its blatant enthusiasms and its brazen effrontery finds a congenial habitat there, not because it is brazen, nor even because it is enthusiastic, but because it supplies a community need. The screaming headline is a mental cocktail. Bellowed forth by a trombone-lunged newsboy, it crashes against the eye, the ear and the brain simultaneously. It whips up tired nerves. It keys the crowd to the keen tension necessary for the doing of the city's business. And the crowd likes it. Fed hourly on mental stimulants, it becomes a slave to its newspapers.

On the morning after Mary Randall's dramatic exit from her uncle's mansion Chicago awoke and clutched at the morning papers with all the eagerness of a drunkard reaching for his dram. A hint of a powerful new thrill lay in the half disclosed first pages. Black headings and "freaked" makeup meant but one thing—a big story.

And Chicago was not disappointed. Occupying the place of honor on the first pages of all of the morning sheets was the announcement of a new assault upon the Vice Trust. To the crowd the name Mary Randall meant nothing. It knew little of her and cared less. But the idea of a young girl, beautiful, socially prominent, immensely wealthy in her own right, declaring war single-handed on a monster so mightily armored and intrenched and so brutally strong as the Vice Trust appealed instantly to the crowd's imagination. In the crowd's thought, at least, the girl became a heroine. And though the man in the street openly wearing an air of cheap cynicism spoke of her as "another crazy reformer" or as a "notoriety-hunting crank," secretly he responded to the enthusiasm of the headline writer who announced her as a "modern Joan of Arc."

Mary had given out the story herself. A simple letter from her to the city editors announcing that she had left her home and all the luxuries that such a home implied and, accompanied only by a maid, had set forth on a war of extermination against the "vice ring" had been sufficient to set every local room in the city in a frenzy. Re-write men and head writers had done the rest. Every newspaper recorded the launching of her adventure with a luxuriance of illustration and a variety of detail that left nothing more to be said on the subject. Mary had counted rather shrewdly on this. She possessed, among her other natural gifts, a keen judgment of news values. She knew, too, the immense power of the press. By enlisting the agencies of publicity behind her she had multiplied her forces a thousand-fold. At the end of her letter Mary had written a modest appeal to the public. Every newspaper printed it under display type. It read as follows:

"TO THE MEN AND WOMEN OF CHICAGO.

"Our city, which should be the heart of American honor, is in the grip of a hideous System. So quietly and surely has this monster worked that our civic blood is poisoned. It feeds upon youth, innocence and purity—all that we as decent citizens love best. I call upon you all to stand by me now in my fight to kill the White Slave Traffic.

"Mary Randall."

Grove Evans read that appeal through and smiled at its naivete. Then he looked across his office to his partner, William Brierly, a younger man with pompadour hair and an habitual air of immense self-satisfaction. Brierly was reading the same story in another newspaper. He, too, looked up and smiled.

"You know this girl, don't you, Grove?" Brierly asked. "By George, she must be interesting. A new kind of female maniac, eh?"

"You've met her," responded Evans. "She was at the Country Club during trophy match last fall. Carries herself like a queen. I remember your raving about her."

"Ah," Brierly's derisive smile faded. "That girl, eh? Say, I saw her make the ninth hole in three. That girl! Say, look here, Grove," he struck the open paper with his palm, "does she mean this stuff?"

Evans lighted a cigarette before replying. "She sure does," he stated finally. "I was at the Randalls when she delivered her ultimatum and took to the war path. Talk about a jolt! After she left us, you could hear the shades of night falling. For ten minutes we sat there exhibiting all the vivacity of a deaf and dumb man at a Quaker prayer-meeting."

Brierly laughed. "Oh, well," he said. "She'll do what all these suffragettes do—run around in a circle, yell herself tired, then marry some fellow and forget it."

He yawned. Evans turned to the huge safe and got out a heavy packet of papers.

"What are you doing, Grove?" Brierly demanded lazily.

"Nothing," responded Evans curtly. "Just looking over some of our shady leases."

"Hello!" said Brierly, getting on his feet. "Are you taking this thing seriously?"

Evans turned with a folded paper in his hand.

"You bet your life I am," he replied. "I know this girl. There's a strain of wild Irish in her and it's my opinion that she's going to raise merry hell!"

The dreamer who had visited the Millville Button Works with the owner of the mill lunched with his friend in the city that day. Quite casually, among other items of interest, Mary Randall's adventure came up for discussion.

"I don't know the girl," said the mill-owner, "but her announcement gives me a fairly good mental picture of her."

"What's your picture?" inquired the journalist.

"A rag and a bone and a hank of hair, one of these raving suffragettes. Since bomb-throwing and burning are not fashionable over here, she's chosen this means of expending her surplus energy."

"My dear friend, you're entirely wrong!"

"What! You've seen her?"

"Oh, no, but I have quite a different mental picture of her. You remember Joan of Arc? Mount her on a charger, hand her a sword of fire and send her forth to fight for Mary Magdalene. That's my idea."

"You've borrowed that from the headline writers," the mill-owner said.

"Not at all. I know the type. A thoughtful young girl, healthy, cultivated and, by the modern miracle, taught how to think. She studies vice conditions in Chicago at first hand and what she sees turns her into a crusader. This girl has spirit. Brought face to face with a great evil, moved by the appeal of helpless womanhood, she throws aside her veneer of false education."

"Unsexed!"

"Yes, if you would say that the crisis in her life unsexed Portia. Or the crisis in France's history unsexed Charlotte Corday."

"You're fond of historical allusions," chided the practical man. "Always the literary man, always the dreamer. This girl is a disturber. She'll unsettle business."

"Ah, there you are. 'Unsettles business.' Did it ever strike you business men that you take yourselves too damn seriously? Any movement, any agitation that 'unsettles business' is ipse facto wrong. You business men have had a hand in the martyring of most of the saints and all of the reformers since time began. And, invariably, you are wrong. Why, you're wrong even about yourselves. You firmly believe that the foundations of the country rest upon you. As a matter of fact, not one per cent of you are producers. You're middlemen, profit shavers, parasites."

Virginia Brooks

"My dear fellow," asked his friend, "where would you be if business men—publishers—didn't buy your wares?"

"Ha," answered the writer, "and where would the publishers be if I and others didn't produce the wares to market? It won't do. The reason the newspapers and magazines of this country are so bad is because most of the publishers are not newspaper men and magazine writers, but merely business men."

"Well, I suppose your Joan of Arc will have to have her fling. Then life will swing back to its same old channels and we'll forget her."

"Yes, she will have her fling and perhaps we'll forget her, but life will not swing back to the same old channel. She'll make a new channel, forgotten though she may be, and it will be a better channel."

*   *   *   *   *

Captain Shammer of the Eighth police district read Mary Randall's open letter through slowly and carefully. When he had finished he lighted a long black cigar from a box that had been sent him by a world famous confidence man. He smoked thoughtfully for some time. Then he put out a heavy hand and, without looking, pressed a white button at the side of his desk.

A sharp-eyed young man opened the captain's door.

"Nick," said the captain, "shut that door a minute and come over here." He pointed to the black newspaper headline.

"Get that?" he demanded.

"Sure, first thing this morning, Captain."

"Well?"

"We should worry."

Captain Shammer rolled his cigar in his mouth. He wasn't exactly satisfied with the answer.

"All right," he agreed finally, "but Nick—"

"Yes, Captain." Nick paused alertly, one hand on the door knob.

"Easy for a while until we see how things break on this."

"Aye, aye, sir!"

"Curtains drawn, you know, and back rooms quiet. Tell the girls to go slow on the piano playing. Did Ike, the dip, come across?"

"Not yet, Captain."

"Pinch him today and give him the cooler. Get me?"

"It's done, cap."

"Close in on the stuss games. Pass the word to go easy."

"I get you."

"Mary Randall, eh?" asked Captain Shammer of vacancy when his aid had gone. "Mary Randall! Well, Mary, you sure have got your nerve with you."

Senator Barker was a member of the Governor's vice investigating committee. The committee had been appointed to frame a minimum wage law for women. He was a person of ponderous bulk and mental equipment. He had slipped into office, not because the people yearned for him, but because there had happened to be a battle on between two factions of his natural political opponents in the fortunate hour he had selected for aspiring to office. Like most other American officeholders he spent his days and nights scheming out ways to continue living at the public's expense. He perused Mary Randall's screed as he sat over his morning grape-fruit.

In an intermission in the committee meeting Senator Barker leaned across the heavy oak table and pointed out the letter to the Rev. Wallace Stillwell.

"Did you see that?" he inquired huskily.

Mr. Stillwell nodded and drew his thin lips together. He was quite young and just now carried the burden of having been called from an obscure country pulpit to a fashionable church in Chicago. He knew that the wealthy man who was his sponsor in this new position was interested in whole blocks of houses whose curtains were always drawn. He had never forgotten a certain phrase that great man had used when he came in his own automobile to bear the young pastor to the new field of his labors.

"We want you, Mr. Stillwell," he had said, "because we believe you to be a safe and sane man, one who will not be swept off his feet by wild-eyed reformers and the anarchistic tendencies of the times."

Mr. Stillwell, therefore, knew why he was wanted in Chicago. The knowledge made him cautious in all things. He thought Senator Barker's question over carefully. Then he nodded calmly.

"Why, yes, Senator," he answered. "One could hardly avoid reading it."

"Well, what about it?"

"Just what do you mean, Senator?"

"You know. What do you think of it, eh?"

"It seems to me," purred the Rev. Wallace Stillwell, "that the whole exploit is worse than fantastic. It is hardly in good taste. Investigations of the kind this girl has undertaken ought to be left to the men."

"That's all right," put in the Senator, gloomily, "but I've noticed lately that the women don't seem to be willing to do that. They want to take a hand in such matters themselves." He leaned back in his chair sadly. "It certainly makes it hard for us politicians."

*   *   *   *   *

A woman of ample girth and a handmade complexion pushed her coffee cup away and lighted a fresh cigarette. She had just finished reading Mary Randall's manifesto. Nature had made her beautiful, but advancing years and too much art had all but destroyed Nature's handicraft. She inhaled the acrid smoke deeply and then raising her voice, called:

"Celeste! You, Celeste!"

A mulatto girl threw open the door, crying:

"Yes, madame?"

"What you doing?"

"Cleaning up."

"Get a bottle of wine. Or did those high rollers guzzle it all last night, the drunken beasts?"

"No, madame. I've saved one for you." She opened the bottle and placed the effervescent liquid before her mistress.

"All right, Celeste. Anybody up yet?"

"I hardly think so, madame."

"Well, I'm up and I wish I wasn't," announced a girl who appeared at that moment coming down the broad staircase. She entered the room.

"Got a head this morning, eh, Nellie?" said the madame, knowingly.

"Yes, I've got a head," replied Nellie sullenly, "and a grouch."

"Make it two, Celeste," said the madame promptly, indicating the bottle. The colored maid poured out another glass of the liquor. Madame threw the paper across the table to the girl.

"There," she said, "that's something that will make you worse."

"Where?" asked the girl, as she caught up the paper.

"Front page, big headlines. You can't miss it."

The girl stepped to the window and pushed aside the heavy curtain. In the morning light she was revealed there petite and charming, despite penciled eyebrows and carmined lips. Her figure was daintily proportioned. There was grace in every line. Her deep brown eyes glowed as she read the words Mary Randall had written.

When she finished reading the girl crumpled the paper in her hand and filled another glass. She lifted the wine slowly.

"Here's to you, Mary Randall," she said.

"That's a rotten toast," said the madame.

"Is it?" replied the girl. "Well, let me tell you something. I'd like to go straight out of this house and find Mary Randall and say to her: 'I'm with you, Mary Randall, and I hope to God you win out.'"

"You don't think of me," whined the older woman. "Look what a knock that reform stuff gives business."

"You!" Nellie's temper flared into a flame. "Say, you ought to be in jail! Now don't start anything you can't finish—" The older woman had got to her feet menacingly. "You don't deserve no pity. You got into this"—she indicated the gaudily furnished house by a gesture, "with your eyes wide open. You picked out this business for yourself. But with me it's different." She leaned across the table defiantly. "Yes, how about me? How about Lottie and Emma—and that poor kid that came here happy because she thought she'd found a decent job? Did we pick out this business? Did we? Not on your life. We walked into a trap and we can't get out. Yes, and there's thousands like us all over this country." She snatched up the bottle and poured more wine. "I'm for you, Mary Randall," she said, raising the glass to the sunlight. "More power to your elbow!"

*   *   *   *   *

Mary Randall read the newspapers in a garret room of a tall lodging house. A pile of letters, in a peculiar shade of dark blue, sealed, stamped and ready for the postoffice, lay in a heap before her. She went through each newspaper carefully, noting the display and studying the "features" of her story that had impressed the newspaper men. At last she laid them down.

"Well, Anna," she said, smiling, addressing her maid. "We've made a good beginning. The town, you see, is interested in us."

Anna's ordinarily impassive face smiled back at her mistress' enthusiasm. Her blue eyes lighted with admiring loyalty. She was blonde, big boned and so strongly built as to look actually formidable. Competency and reserve power fairly radiated from her. Her voice betrayed her Scandinavian ancestry.

"Ya-as," she said, "and in another week they'll be fighting for us."

Mary got up from her chair and went to the window, threw it wide open and looked out on the city. She saw its myriad lights rimming the shore of the inland sea. She heard its roar—deep, passionate, powerful. In her imagination she laid her ear close to the city's heart and she heard it beat strong and true. The smile had left her face and a prayer formed itself silently on her lips. The revery lasted only a moment.

"And now," she said, "for the next movement in the battle." She indicated the letters. "There's our ammunition, Anna," she said. "Mail them. I've picked you for a great honor. You're to open the engagement with a fusillade of bombshells."

CHAPTER XI

A BOMB FOR MR. GROGAN

The telephone in the outer office of the Lake City Telephone Company rang insistently. Miss Masters, the stenographer, after the fashion of stenographers, let it ring. At length the telephone gave vent to a long, shrill, despairing appeal and was silent. Then, and then only, did Miss Masters lay aside the bundle of letters she was sorting and pick up the receiver.

"Yes?" she said. "Well, what is it?"

Apparently a voice responded.

"Speak a little louder, please," the girl said impersonally. "I can't hear a single word you're saying."

More words from the outside poured through the receiver.

"Yes." Miss Masters nodded mechanically. "Yes, this is the main office of the Lake City Electrical Company. What?"

There was another pause.

"This is Miss Masters at the 'phone,—yes—yes—I'm the stenographer. What's that? Private secretary? Yes, I am Mr.

John Boland's private secretary. No, our president, Mr. Harry Boland, has not come downtown yet. We are expecting him at any moment."

A red-headed office boy stuck an inquisitive head through the door.

"Who's that," he demanded, "someone for the boss?"

Miss Masters merely motioned him to silence.

"Yes," she went on, "his father, Mr. John Boland, will be in some time during the morning. Who shall I say called?"

The girl waited for the answer and hung up the receiver.

"Who is it, Miss Masters?" inquired the boy.

"Well, Dickey, I don't think it's any of your business," retorted Miss Masters good-naturedly. "But, for fear you'll burst with curiosity, I'll say that it's Mr. Martin Druce."

"Happy as a crab this morning, ain't you?" jeered the boy. "Well, you want to look out for that geezer, Druce. He's a devil with the girls."

Miss Masters made a face at him and the boy, whistling derisively, disappeared through the door, not failing to slam it loudly after him.

Miss Masters resumed her letter sorting. The door opened slowly. A man entered with his hat over his eyes. His hands were deep in his pockets and he chewed a despondent looking cigar. Had the reader been present he would have recognized him instantly, despite his unaccustomed air of lugubriousness, as our old friend, Mr. Michael Grogan.

"Good morning, Mr. Grogan," said Miss Masters cordially.

Grogan made no reply. The girl went on with her work. Then as if communing with herself she said: "And yet they say the Irish are always polite."

"Eh?" said Grogan, rousing himself, "what's that?"

Miss Masters vouchsafed no reply. She merely laughed. Grogan, conscious that he was being chaffed, stared at her. He was pleased with what he saw. He found Miss Masters handsome. Her office dress, slit at the bottom and displaying at this moment a neat ankle, was ruched about the neck and sleeves. It was a rather elaborate dress for a stenographer, but John Boland was a vain man and liked to have the employes he kept close about him maintain the appearance of prosperity. In fact, he paid these particular employes well with the explicit understanding that they would keep their appearance up to his standard.

"You're making light of me gray hairs, I see," said Mr. Grogan, smiling.

"Well," said the girl, "I said good morning to you and you didn't even grunt in reply."

"The top of the morning to you, Miss Masters," said Grogan, hastening to remedy his oversight and removing his hat with an ornate bow.

"Sure, and I'm wishing you the same and many of them," replied the girl.

Mr. Grogan bowed again and added:

"And, if I have failed in the politeness due a lady, I begs

yer pardon."

"You're forgiven, Mr. Grogan," replied Miss Masters, resuming her work.

Grogan returned to his meditations. He was regarding his mutilated cigar ruefully when Miss Masters observed:

"If all of the millionaires were as thorough gentlemen as you are, Mr. Grogan, we wouldn't have any labor unions."

The word millionaire seemed to sting Grogan.

"I'll thank you," he said abruptly, "to leave me out of the millionaire class."

"Why, Mr. Grogan," said the girl, surprised, "I thought you'd like that!"

"So would I—wanst," retorted Grogan, "but now when any one says 'you millionaire,' faith, I get ready to dodge a brick."

"I should think it would be pleasant to know you had a million dollars." There was a note of envy in the girl's voice.

Grogan rose slowly, walked to the desk and leaned across it confidentially.

"So it always was," he said sententiously, "but now they're beginning to ask, 'Where did you get it?'"

"Oh," said the girl.

"It's not 'Oh,' I'm saying," said Grogan, "it's 'Ouch!'"

"Something's disturbing you, eh?"

"Something—and somebody. 'Tis a girl."

"Oh, Mr. Grogan!"

"Whist!" retorted Mr. Grogan, "You don't get me meaning. It's not the kind you buy ice cream sodies for. No! This lady has a club in her fist and a punch in both elbows."

"For you?"

"I suspicion so, and I'm oneasy in me mind."

"It's silly to worry, Mr. Grogan," said Miss Masters, "sit down and look over the papers." She extended a morning newspaper, smiling.

"I may as well." Grogan took up the paper and selected a chair.

"Stirring times in Chicago, just now," said the young woman.

"They're stirring, all right," Grogan agreed. "They're too stirring. What I want is peace. I'd like to pass the rest of my days in quiet—quiet—and—"

The sentence expired on his lips as he stared at the front page of the paper held open in his hands.

"What's the matter, Mr. Grogan," said Miss Masters starting up, alarmed.

Grogan wiped his forehead and moistened his lips.

"Nothing," he said, "it's hot and I'm—I'm—"

He threw the newspaper on the floor.

"Here," he said, "give me another newspaper."

The girl picked up another paper from the heap on the corner of the desk and passed it across to him. Grogan looked at the headlines.

"Help—murder," he cried. Then he cast the paper on the floor and got to his feet abruptly.

"Mr. Grogan," asked the girl, "what is the matter?"

"I asked for quiet," Grogan replied, picking up the papers and shaking them angrily, "and on the front page of this paper is a letter written and signed by Mary Randall."

"And why should Mary Randall disturb you?"

"Do you know she writes to me?"

"Writes to you?"

"She does."

"What does she say?"

"Everything—and then some," was the grim response. "Don't laugh!" he ordered. "Here's one of the last of them." Grogan took a dark blue envelope from his pocket, extracted a single sheet of the same color and read.

"Michael Grogan:—Do you remember what your old Irish mother said to you when you left Old Erin to seek your fortune in the new world? She said: 'Mike, me boy, don't soil your hands with dirty money.' Mary Randall."

"Don't soil your hands with dirty money," repeated Miss Masters.

"That's a nice billy dux to find beside your plate at breakfast, ain't it now?" demanded Grogan. Then after a pause he murmured half to himself,

"Me old Irish mother, God bless her, with her white hair and her sweet Connemara face! I can see her now, just as she stood there that day in the door of our cabin when I went off up the road, a slip of a boy, with a big bag of oatmeal over me shoulder—one shirt and me Irish fighting spirit. That was me capital in life, that and her blessing. She's sleeping there now, and the shamrock is growing over her—"

Grogan stopped. His voice had grown husky.

"Say," he demanded turning on Miss Masters abruptly, "why don't you make me stop? Don't you see I'm breaking me heart?"

The girl had really been moved. "I can't," she said, "because—" She got out her powder puff and proceeded hastily to decorate her nose. She was still engaged in this operation when the telephone rang. Grogan started.

"What's that?" he demanded.

"Why, it's only the telephone. What is the matter with you, Mr. Grogan?"

"I dunno," responded Grogan despondently, "I'm as nervous as a girl in a peek-a-boo waist."

The telephone rang again.

"Why don't you answer that?" demanded Grogan sharply.

"I will," replied the girl, "but there's no great rush, is there?"

"Yes there is," insisted Grogan, "I can't bear the suspense."

The young woman laughed and picked up the receiver.

"Lake City Electrical Company," she said. "What? Who is it, please."

Grogan, who had continued pacing up and down the office, stopped and made wild gestures to Miss Masters. Covering the mouthpiece of the instrument so she would not be heard, the girl asked.

"What is it, Mr. Grogan?"

"Whist!" replied Grogan, "If that is Mary Randall on the wire there, I've gone to Alaska. I've given all me money away and I'm living on snow balls."

Miss Masters smiled and replied with assurance: "This isn't Mary Randall."

"Thank God for that," breathed Grogan.

"Hello," went on Miss Masters into the telephone. "Oh, you're long distance? Well?"

There was a pause.

"I'm sorry, but Mr. Harry Boland hasn't come downtown yet."

"He may be in any moment—shall I—"

She broke off sharply as Harry himself came in the door drawing off his gloves.

"Wait! Just a moment please," she went on. "He has just come in."

"Someone for me, Miss Masters?" the young man inquired, hanging up his hat on a rack by the door. Without waiting for a reply he turned to Grogan. "Good morning, Mike."

"'Tis a fine day—I hope," returned Grogan cautiously.

"Yes, someone calling you, Mr. Boland," broke in Miss Masters.

"Don't want to talk to anyone," said the young man curtly.

"Hello, hello," continued Miss Masters at the telephone. "Hello, long distance? Mr. Boland is too busy—"

"Wait, please," interrupted Harry quickly, "did you say 'long distance?'"

Miss Masters nodded. "Just a moment," she said into the telephone.

"Yes, Mr. Boland," she said. "It's a long distance. Some one wants to talk to you in—Millville, Illinois."

CHAPTER XII

BAD NEWS FROM MILLVILLE

The word Millville had an instantaneous effect on Harry Boland. It was, in fact, the most pleasant sound he had heard in days. Upon returning to Chicago after his lover-like interview with Patience Welcome he had dispatched a long letter to her. To this he had received no reply. Then he wrote two letters in one day. Neither of them had been answered. Thoroughly disturbed now, but too busy to leave Chicago himself, Harry had sent his confidential man, John Clark, to Millville to learn, if possible, the cause of Patience's silence.

While Harry stood eagerly waiting for the 'phone Miss Masters was busy getting the long distance connection.

"All right, Mr. Boland," she said at last, "here's your party." Then into the telephone she continued: "Yes—Mr. Boland is here waiting. He will talk to Millville. Hello—hello—Millville? Hello!" She handed Harry the instrument.

"I wouldn't answer that 'phone for a thousand dollars," put in Grogan dolefully.

"Hello—hello!" exclaimed Harry.

A shrill whistle rent the air and Grogan jumped hysterically.

"What's that?" he demanded.

"The postman's whistle," replied Miss Masters calmly, represssing a smile as she started for the outer door.

"Hello, Millville, hello," called Harry Boland, not getting his connection.

Grogan beckoned Miss Masters to his side. "If there's a letter there for me in an envelope like this," he said producing the dark blue letter from his pocket, "you keep it."

"Really?" Miss Masters now smiled openly.

"Keep it," reiterated Grogan, "don't show it to me or I'll climb up the side of the building and jump off."

Miss Masters thoroughly amused vanished into the hall. Meanwhile Harry Boland was talking to Millville.

"Millville?" he said. "Yes this is Harry Boland. Oh!" He paused with a distinct note of disappointment in his voice. "Oh, it's you, Clark? Yes I know—You've something to report about the Welcomes."

"The Welcome family," said Grogan, pricking up his ears.

"All right, I'm listening," Harry went on. "Yes, I get you."

"Look at that now," continued Grogan reflectively.

"No, no, you needn't wait there any longer—All right."

He hung up the receiver.

"Asking your pardon," ventured Grogan, "may I take the liberty of an old friend to inquire what Mr. Boland wants with a bum family like the Welcomes—"

"Just a moment, Mike," interrupted Harry putting out his hand imperatively. "You're speaking of the girl I mean to marry."

Grogan gaped at the young man.

"I am?" he gasped.

"You are," replied the other. He rose to his feet and turned tranquilly toward Grogan. "Now what are you going to say?" he inquired.

"Nothing," said Grogan, too surprised to talk.

"All right," replied Harry pointedly.

"But the old man is no good," hazarded Grogan. "Tom Welcome is a worthless—"

"He's dead, Mike," interrupted Harry.

"What?" This was a day of surprises for Grogan.

"He's dead," repeated Harry, "died the night we left Millville."

"Well," Grogan's manner had changed. "There were some good points about the man, after all. I've heard he'd never take a drink alone—if he could avoid it."

"And the Welcome family has moved away," Harry went on.

"Where?"

"No one knows. I've been too busy to investigate myself so I sent Clark to locate them."

"Aha," said Grogan. "Then it was Clark you were talking to?"

"Of course," replied Harry impatiently, "didn't you hear?"

"Yes, yes, but—" Grogan broke off abruptly. "Say, didn't that fat fellow who was going to be a detective, the fellow who nearly killed me riding on his grocery wagon, didn't he know anything?"

"He's left Millville, too."

"What!" exclaimed Grogan incredulously. "Do you mean to say a bunch like that can drop out of a town like Millville without anyone knowing where they've gone?"

"I'm not telling you. The facts speak for themselves," said Harry.

Both men were silent.

"Mike," said young Boland suddenly.

"Yes," responded Grogan.

"You were married?"

The Irishman was too surprised by the question to answer.

"I've heard you speak about your wife," Harry insisted.

Grogan still vouchsafed no answer. He stood staring at Boland.

"I've heard you speak of your wife, Norah," repeated Harry, "in a way that made me feel how sacred her memory was to you. She married you, a husky young Irish laborer in the mills, and how that little woman worked for you, toiling, saving, scrimping, tending the babies as they came! How you worshiped her, and big man as you were, how a word from her would make you kneel at her feet. You held her in your arms when the little mounds were raised in the church yard—"

Grogan listened in silence, deeply moved. He put out his hand and grasped Harry's firmly.

"That's the way I love Patience Welcome, Mike," went on Harry, "just as you loved Norah McGuire."

"Well," broke in Grogan huskily, "I didn't know—I—" He turned suddenly and demanded, "Well then, why in hell don't you find her?"

"I'm going to try."

"And I'll help ye!"

"Good old Mike," said Harry, putting his arm around Grogan's shoulders, "Aha, you can't beat the Irish!"

"Yes, you can," responded Grogan, "but they won't stay beaten."

The conversation was interrupted by the entrance of Boland senior. He hung up his hat, took off his gloves and rubbed his hands together.

"Ah," he said, "good morning Harry—Mike."

"Morning, Governor," returned Harry tersely. Grogan acknowledged the salutation with a grunt.

"Have Miss Masters make out a lease for that house in South Twelfth street," went on the elder Boland briskly. He laid some papers on the table. "Here is the copy of the present lease with the necessary changes noted."

"Who's the lessee?" inquired Harry carelessly.

"Carter Anson."

"What!" exclaimed Harry in amazement.

"Well, well, what's the matter?" demanded the father.

"Ask Mike," said the young man turning with a smile to Grogan.

"I refuse to answer any questions," declared Grogan. "'Tis a little rule I learned in politics."

"Carter Anson is going to be indicted by the grand jury," Harry informed his father.

"Ah," said John Boland, "you've been reading the yellow journals."

"They're yellow," conceded Harry, "because they contain so many golden truths."

"Mary Randall, please write," sneered the elder Boland.

"Stop! No!" Grogan, who had been sitting down jumped to

his feet in protest. The others looked at him in astonishment. He sat down again shamefacedly. "I don't want Mary Randall to write to me," he admitted dolefully.

"What's come over you, Grogan?" inquired John Boland sharply.

"A blue envelope—a sheet of blue paper with words on it, and—I've got a pain in the back of my neck." Grogan brought forth the blue letter again and gazed at it gloomily.

"You're crazy," John Boland informed him curtly. Then he turned to Harry. "Look here, my boy," he said, "don't be a fool—"

"He's your son," interrupted Grogan chuckling.

"Keep quiet, Mike. You know, Harry, I own that property with Mike here, and—"

Grogan interrupted again. "Look here, John Boland," he inquired, "how much will you give me for my share?"

"Two thousand dollars."

"It's yours," said Grogan.

"Why it's worth double that!" exclaimed John Boland.

"Never mind that. It's yours," repeated Grogan. "I'll give two thousand for my peace of mind any day."

"Are you crazy?"

"Not yet—but I'm headed that way. Take it at two thousand and I'll love you, John."

"All right."

"But, Governor," protested Harry, "don't you know—"

"Now don't let a fool reform wave scare you," burst out the father irritably. "Did you ever see a vice investigation get anywhere? Never! Just a lot of talk and—letters."

Miss Masters appeared with a package of letters in her hands. "Mail, Mr. Boland," she said. She began sorting the letters. "Four for you, Mr. Boland," she went on, "and a special for Mr. Harry Boland."

Grogan had been watching her intently. He breathed deeply and muttered: "Sure and I'm an old fool. Why should I be afraid of letters? Who could write—"

Miss Masters interrupted. "And one for you, Mr. Grogan," she said casually.

Grogan dropped into his chair crying: "Help!" Then cautiously he took the letter from Miss Masters. The envelope was white and he heaved a sigh of relief.

"What the deuce ails you this morning, Grogan?" demanded John Boland irritated.

"I'm getting second sight," returned Grogan gloomily, "and I don't like it."

"Oh, don't be a fool." John Boland began opening his mail. "All this investigating," he continued, "this talk of a minimum wage law, is just talk and that's all. Now take this crazy woman—Mary Randall—"

While he spoke he had opened a letter containing a second

enclosure. It was an envelope of a peculiar shape and its color was dark blue.

CHAPTER XIII

THE READER MEETS
ANOTHER OLD ACQUAINTANCE

The sight of the blue envelope had transfixed Grogan. He stood staring at it like a man in the presence of a ghost.

"The blue envelope, again," he cried. "A harpoon for you, John."

John Boland made no reply. He reached for his paper knife, ripped open the envelope and drew forth a sheet of blue note paper. He read with a gathering frown what had been written on it. Then he reread it, muttering under his breath.

"Does it hurt you much, John?" inquired Grogan, enjoying the other's discomfiture.

For answer the elder Boland scrutinized Grogan over his glasses.

"What do you know about this, Mike?" he demanded.

"Only that I got one of those blue bombs myself this morning," retorted Grogan.

"Listen to this." John Boland flourished the envelope angrily. "'The owner of property who leases same to vice is morally responsible for the crimes committed on his premises. Mary Randall.'"

He turned to Grogan. "What do you think of that?" he asked.

"She's hit home," replied Grogan grimly.

"Damn her, for a brazen busybody," blurted Boland angrily. "Why doesn't she mind her own business?"

Meanwhile Harry was opening an envelope the exact counterpart of his father's. He read the note twice and stood considering its import.

"Another of 'em?" said the elder Boland. "Well, what's yours, Harry?"

"Mine?—Oh,—mine—why," the young man faltered.

"Well, well, can't you speak?" demanded the father irritably.

Harry returned no direct reply. Opening his note he read:

"We count on young men like you, Harry Boland, to lead the fight we are making to save our Little Lost Sisters. Mary Randall."

"Now," chuckled Grogan, "you know how I felt when I got my little blue envelope this morning." As he spoke he tore off the end of the envelope which he had held unnoticed. Inserting his finger and thumb into the envelope he went on:

"Do you know, I never did like the color of blue—"

He broke off as he lowered his eyes to the enclosure he had brought out. It was another blue letter. Grogan started up and jerked out the note. Holding it at arms' distance he read:

"The strength of Ireland is in the purity of her sons and daughters. Mary Randall."

The three men stood staring at each other in amazement.

"Mary Randall." John Boland broke the silence with a sneer.

"Mary Randall," repeated Harry quietly.

"Oh you Mary Randall!" put in Grogan with just a touch of admiration in his voice. "She's the lady champion light-weight. Three knock-outs in three minutes. 'Tis a world's record!" He turned to the elder Boland. "Does the punch she gave you hurt much?" he inquired.

Boland glared at Grogan. "Who the devil is Mary Randall?" he demanded.

"I've never met her," replied Harry. "She's a member of the wealthy Randall family. Her mother died when she was young and I understand she was brought up very quietly."

"Do you know her, Miss Masters," persisted Boland.

The girl was startled, "I—why—I?" she hesitated.

"Yes—yes," said Harry, "do you know her?"

The girl still hesitated and Grogan broke in.

"You're a woman, Miss Masters," he said, "you ought to know all the feminine quirks. Now it's up to you. Who's

Mary Randall?"

"Mary Randall is a wealthy girl," said Miss Masters calmly. "She has grown weary of the foolish methods you men have employed in attacking the vice problem. Convinced of your total incompetence she has started out really to do something."

"What does she want?" snorted John Boland.

"She said in a printed letter," replied Miss Masters, "that she wanted to put several property owners and crooked senators in jail."

Grogan was impressed by this statement.

"Do you want to buy the rest of my South Side property, John?" he inquired of Boland.

"Doesn't she know she's disturbing business?" asked Boland of Miss Masters, ignoring Grogan.

"Mary Randall also said," the girl replied, "that the greatest business in the world is that of redeeming 'Little Lost Sisters.'"

"You see, you see," said Grogan, "the farther you go, John, the more punches you get."

"I haven't time to bother with this foolishness," said Boland. "I've got a big contract on with the Simmons people."

He went to the door of his son's office.

"Come on Harry—you too Mike. Come in, Miss Masters, and take down this contract."

The three men started toward the door. As Grogan passed Miss Masters he whispered: "Young woman, if any more blue skyrockets come for me, play the hose on them."

"Very well," said the girl, smiling.

Having secured her notebook she started toward the inner office when a smartly dressed young man entered.

"Hello girlie," he said, intercepting her.

"Good morning," replied Miss Masters primly. "What's your business?"

"Oh, just like that, eh?" said the youth.

"Yes," replied the girl sharply. "What do you want?"

"Mr. John Boland."

"You can't see him now. He's busy."

There was a sharp, impatient call from the inner office.

"Yes sir, I'm coming," replied the girl.

"Well, be quick about it," returned the voice. "Do you think I can wait all day?"

"That's John Boland, isn't it?" inquired the man eagerly.

Miss Masters nodded assent.

"Well, tell him—"

"I'm sorry," broke in the girl, "but he's busy. He won't

see anyone."

"Well then, tell him when you can that Martin Druce called."

"Martin Druce!" Miss Masters kept her eyes on the blank page before her, but she made no effort to make a memorandum of the name. She added slowly:

"You called on the 'phone this morning."

"I sure did." Druce, with the familiarity of an old acquaintance, began toying with the silver vanity box Miss Randall wore suspended from her neck. "Say," he went on insinuatingly, "you have the sweetest voice—"

"Better tell me why you want to see Mr. Boland," she said quietly taking the vanity box from him and putting him at a distance. At the same time she smiled at him archly.

"Just want to renew a lease—the Cafe Sinister."

"Oh," said the girl, "I've heard of it."

"It's some swell place," replied Druce with pride.

"Yes?" said the girl. She pantomimed counting money. "Yes, as long as you can keep the police asleep."

"What in—what the deuce do you mean?" Druce inquired quickly.

Miss Masters shrugged her shoulders. Again she smiled at him archly.

"Oh, you're wise, eh?" Druce laughed. He felt that he was on familiar ground with this girl. There was that in her manner that indicated the wisdom of the demi-monde. He thought he had placed her.

"You're wise, eh?" he repeated. The girl had maneuvered to place a table between them. He leaned against the table and placed a hand on hers.

"Why does a fine looker like you spend her life pounding a typewriter?"

"Would you advise a change?"

"You could make a hundred a week in the cabarets," declared Druce admiringly.

"Perhaps," replied Miss Masters. She picked up her notebook and started for the inner office. "But I know where that road leads."

Druce was daunted with this reply. It wasn't at all what he had expected.

"Oh," he jeered, "you're one of the goody-goody kind, are you? Fare you well. I'll see you in church Sunday."

The girl was now at the inner office door. She turned and eyed Druce narrowly.

"Thank you," she replied without anger.

"Perhaps, some day, I'll see you wearing stripes and looking through iron bars!"

The door shut swiftly behind her, leaving Druce staring at the panels.

"What do you know about that," he spoke aloud, though there was no one in the outer office to hear him.

"Never mind, kid—you're no boob, anyway." He turned on his heel and walked out.

CHAPTER XIV

IN WHICH THE WOLF IS BITTEN BY THE LAMB

John Boland was a very capable business man. He possessed the combination of shrewdness, ability to grasp and marshal details, and that utter selfishness which the world from time immemorial has rewarded with huge accumulations of money. He had one of those minds which find their recreation in intrigue. Unembarrassed by a conscience and unhampered by scruples he drove directly to his goal—success.

As head of the Electric Trust Boland was compelled to be at once a financier and a politician. The faculties for success in both fields are closely allied; in both Boland was eminently triumphant. Sitting in his office day after day, unmoved by events that might have disturbed other men and unstirred by emotions that might have turned other men from their paths, he looked out over the city and "played his game" with all the cold impassiveness of a gambler operating an infallible system in roulette. No detail was too small to escape his notice, no agent too ignoble to serve his purpose.

These facts are mentioned to explain the relationship that existed between John Boland and Martin Druce. In these two men, the social extremes of the city met—Boland, the financial power and leading citizen; Druce, the dive keeper and social outcast. They met because Boland wished it. Druce was one of the creatures that he could and often did use in his business.

Although ostensibly ignorant of the very existence of Druce, Boland in reality had the man often in his thoughts. He kept these thoughts hidden in that inner chamber of his mind from which, from time to time, emerged those inspirations that had made his name a by-word on La Salle street for supernatural astuteness. Not even the most intimate of his coworkers guessed them.

For nearly a month now Druce had been calling at Boland's offices intent on obtaining a renewal of his lease to the Cafe Sinister. During that entire month he had never been able to obtain even a word with the master financier. Boland had purposely refused to grant the interview so frequently requested by Druce not because he had any repugnance against doing business with the dive keeper but because to his mind there had never appeared any good reason why he should grant that interview. He played the waiting game with Druce because he had found by profitable experience that the waiting game paid John Boland best. The time might come when he would be able to use so excellent a tool as Druce to its best advantage. Boland was waiting calmly for that time. If Druce suffered in the interim John Boland was unable to see how that was any of his concern. In fact, Boland figured, the more Druce suffered, the keener a tool he would be for his purposes.

Druce guessed something of this. He too possessed a mind adapted to intrigue. Therefore every rebuff from Boland found him undaunted. He knew that his time must come. He called at Boland's offices again and again, smiling always in the face of denial.

Of late a new incentive for calling at the Electric Trust's offices had developed for Druce. This was furnished by Miss Masters. The girl's charming looks had aroused the man's curiosity and cunning. Her air of worldly wisdom, her alternate repulses and advances, had stirred him as he had rarely been stirred before. In his eagerness to possess her he almost lost sight of the main object of his visits.

But whether by accident or design Druce was never able to get a word with the girl alone. She was always, save on the sole occasion of his last visit, either engaged with Harry Boland's dictation, or, if in the outer office, chaperoned by Harry Boland's red-headed office boy. One day Druce met Red in the lower corridor of the Electric Trust building. The boy grinned knowingly at him and yelled as he hurried by.

"I'll be back in a minute."

"Don't hurry on my account," answered Druce, but at the moment it came to him that Red's chaperonage of Miss Masters might not be entirely accidental.

Druce stepped into the elevator and was let out at the Electric Trust's offices. He entered and found the offices empty.

"Hang the little fool," he said, "she doesn't know which side her bread is—"

"Meaning whom?" inquired Miss Masters' saccharine voice.

Druce turned quickly and saw Miss Masters coming from the inner office. He was impressed by the attractiveness of her dress.

"Where does she get all the glad rags?" he demanded of himself. "Maybe old Boland—"

"Who's a little fool?" persisted Miss Masters.

"Nobody," returned Druce. "Just talking to myself. Mr. Boland's out or busy, I suppose?"

"Yes, Mr. Boland's out," replied Miss Masters. She sat down at a typewriter and inserted a sheet of paper in the machine. "He left a message for you, however. He told me this morning that if you called I should ask you to 'phone him about twelve o'clock. He'll try to see you then for a moment."

"All right," said Druce, "thanks." But he made no move to go. He watched the girl as she hammered the typewriter keys. Presently she looked up at him inquiringly.

This to Druce appeared to be a direct offer to open a conversation. He hastened to take advantage of it.

"Yes," he replied in his most ingratiating manner, drawing near her. "I want to talk to you. I have been dying to speak to you alone, girlie—"

The girl rose from her chair and picked up her notebook.

"Oh, Mr. Druce," she said.

"Yes, girlie."

Miss Masters opened the notebook and took a lead pencil from the shining rolls of her hair.

"I have to keep a record of all callers," said the girl unexpectedly. "Mr. Boland is very particular about it. Let me see, your name is Martin Druce?"

She wrote the name into her book and showed it to him.

"I have the name correctly, haven't I, Mr. Druce?" she went on.

"Rather tardy with your duties, aren't you?" inquired Druce with a smile. "I've been coming here for some days now and you haven't wanted to put me into your book before."

"Perhaps," replied the girl, "I haven't noticed you."

Druce was sure now that he was beginning a flirtation with her.

"And your business?" continued the girl.

"Oh, Boland knows my business," replied Druce, with an air of carelessness.

"No doubt he does, but I don't. And how can I keep my records properly if I don't know? I can't bother Mr. Boland with these details. What is your business?"

"Why—ah—" hesitated Druce. "Live stock."

"What kind of live stock?" persisted Miss Masters, preparing to write down his answer.

"Eh!" Druce began to feel that he was being badgered.

"What kind of live stock do you deal in?"

"See here," snarled Druce, "what are you trying to do?"

Miss Masters' answer was perfectly calm. "I am trying," she said, "to find out what kind of live stock you deal in, Mr. Druce."

"Forget it!"

"Are you ashamed to tell me?"

Druce turned on the girl as though stung.

"Why should I be ashamed?" he blustered. He moved toward the door.

"I'll know that," replied Miss Masters, "when you tell me what kind of live stock you deal in."

There was a stern quality in Miss Masters' voice that Druce had noticed in the voice of a district attorney with whom he had once had an unpleasant interview. The man was a coward. He wanted to be off.

"Every kind," he blurted. "Good day."

A moment later he found himself in the hallway. "Red," the office boy, had just come from the elevator.

"What's the trouble, Druce?" demanded the boy. "You look pale around the gills."

"You go to hell, you little rat," retorted Druce, and without waiting for the elevator vanished down the steps, with the jeering laughter of the boy ringing in his ears.

CHAPTER XV

THE SEARCH BEGINS FOR THE LOST SISTER

There was nothing in Miss Masters' manner after Druce had made his hasty departure to indicate that she felt any thrills of triumph over the completeness of the dive keeper's rout. On the contrary she seemed unaccountably depressed. She sat down at her typewriter thinking deeply. Presently her meditations were disturbed.

The door opened quietly. A man entered who, in spite of the shabbiness of his clothing, his emaciation and the haggardness of his features the reader would have had no difficulty in recognizing. He was Harvey Spencer. He stood in the open door looking at the girl uncertainly. She took him in in a glance.

"Good morning," she said sympathetically. "You are looking for someone here?"

"I was," replied Harvey enigmatically, "but he's gone."

"Gone?" repeated the girl.

"Yes," replied the caller quickly, "perhaps you can give me some information. That man, who stepped in here a moment

Virginia Brooks

ago—you know who he is?"

"Yes," replied the girl, "his name is Martin Druce."

"That's his name, yes—what's his business?"

"Live stock, he says," replied Miss Masters in some surprise.

"You know where he lives?"

"No. Won't you sit down?"

"I can't. I'm following him."

The girl was bewildered. "Are you a detective?" she inquired.

The question produced an extraordinary effect on the young man. He threw up his head and gave vent to a short, sharp exclamation.

"Ha!" he said. "No," he went on, "I once thought I was a detective, but I woke up." Then he started for the door. "Thank you," he said. As he reached for the knob he reeled and clutched at the wall for support. Miss Masters started toward him.

"Come," she said, "sit down. Aren't you feeling ill? Let me get you a glass of water."

She drew a glass full from a cooler and carried it to the young man.

"It's warm," she said, "you're exhausted."

Harvey gulped the contents of the glass, and looked at Miss Masters mournfully.

"Thanks," he said. "Yes—mighty warm."

"Looking for a job?" inquired Miss Masters.

"I ought to be," was the reply.

"Why aren't you?"

"Because," Harvey's despondency deepened, "I'm looking for a girl."

"A girl from down state?"

"How did you know that?"

"Why," replied Miss Masters, "you don't belong to Chicago. Your clothes tell me that. And the girl—she was from your own town?"

"Yes."

"Tell me about it?" Miss Masters' manner was friendly. She drew a chair and sat down opposite the young man. Harvey was so moved by this unlocked for sympathy that tears filled his eyes.

"Her name," he said huskily, "was Elsie Welcome. She ran away. Her father had beaten her. On the night she left the father died. We were to have been married. I learned that she had come to Chicago with this man—Martin Druce. I follo-wed her. For days I have tramped the streets. Today I caught a glimpse of Druce as he entered an elevator in this building. I had just reached here when I lost sight of him."

The door behind him opened slowly. Miss Masters looked up to see a gray haired woman enter. She wore a waist and skirt of dead black with a little old fashioned black bonnet. Her face was sweet with motherliness, but drawn with sorrow and exhaustion.

"Harvey," she said.

Harvey turned and hurried to her side.

"I saw you come in here, Harvey," the woman went on, "so I followed. I hope we're not intruding Miss—"

"Masters is my name," responded the stenographer quickly.

"This is the girl's mother," said Harvey. "This is Mrs. Martha Welcome."

Miss Masters hastened to bring another chair.

"And your daughter," she asked quickly, "have you—"

"I—I don't think there was anything wrong in Elsie's going away," interrupted Mrs. Welcome. "She wasn't happy and her father—"

"Her father beat her," said Harvey wrathfully.

"Harvey," chided Mrs. Welcome, "Tom's dead. He wasn't a bad man, Miss Masters. He lost his courage when he lost his invention."

"I understand," said Miss Masters sympathetically. "You haven't heard anything from your lost girl?"

"No," replied Mrs; Welcome sadly, "not a word. Patience and I and Harvey came to the city hoping to find her—"

"Patience?"

"She's my other daughter," replied Mrs. Welcome, "two years older. Elsie was my baby." Her voice broke.

"I'm wondering," she went on in subdued tones, "if she's all right. I've prayed, too. Seems as though I've prayed every minute that God would bring my baby back to me. You don't think it makes any difference, do you, Miss Masters, even if we are in a great, noisy city? God is here, too, isn't he?"

She put out her hand impulsively and Miss Masters took it into her own cool palm.

"Yes, God is here," she replied reverently, "though sometimes it is hard to have faith and believe it."

Harvey had walked away and stood looking out at the door.

"Here's Patience," he said suddenly.

Patience Welcome entered almost immediately. She was dressed in the same somber black as her mother. She wore a heavy veil pushed back from the brim of her hat. Harvey presented her to Miss Masters.

"I've good news for you, mother," exclaimed Patience after acknowledging the introduction. "I've got a place in that office I went into when I left you. I begin work tomorrow. Then when I came out and missed you I was terribly frightened, but the elevator man told me you had come in here. And so I found you."

"Your mother has been telling me something about the search for your sister," said Miss Masters. "Perhaps I may be able to help you. Could you tell me something about it?"

"Thank you," replied Patience, "we need help. It seems as if we had exhausted all our own resources. But we mustn't stop now. Mother is worn out."

"Perhaps," said Miss Masters, "it would be better if this young man should take your mother home. You and I may be able to talk the situation over more confidentially if we are alone."

"You think you can help us?" inquired Patience eagerly.

Miss Masters was thoughtful. "Yes," she said, "I believe I have unusual facilities for helping you. I know a great deal about Chicago—"

"Then," said Patience, "I'll put our case in your hands. I know I can trust you. Somehow, I feel better already."

She took Miss Masters' hands in her own, confidently.

"Yes," returned Miss Masters, a little tremulously, "you can trust me."

Harvey in the meantime had helped Mrs. Welcome with her wraps and was leading her toward the door.

"I'll follow in a little while," said Patience, as the two passed out the door. "I'll be home in time for supper."

"Now," said Miss Masters, after Harvey and Mrs. Welcome were gone, "first tell me if you have any money."

Patience hesitated. Such a question coming from a stranger embarrassed her.

"Yes," she said slowly, "I think we have enough money.

Harvey brought fifty dollars with him and Mother was given some money by a man who came to our aid, in Millville—"

"Millville?" interrupted Miss Masters.

"Yes," continued Patience, "that is the town we live in. The man's name was Dudley—"

"Dudley!"

Patience looked at Miss Masters in surprise. "You know him?" she asked.

Miss Masters hesitated. "The name seems familiar," she said.

"He was a stranger in Millville," Patience went on. "My mother wired to her sister, Sarah, for money after Elsie left us and my father died. My aunt sent us forty dollars."

There was a pause after this explanation, then Miss Masters went on hesitatingly.

"Forgive me, Miss Welcome," she said, "if I speak plainly to you. Were there any strangers in Millville about the time your sister went away?"

"Strangers?" repeated Patience.

"Any attractive young men," pursued Miss Masters.

"Why—why—I—" stammered Patience in confusion.

"There were, I see."

"You don't think my sister—" burst out Patience.

"Forgive me," interrupted Miss Masters, "but when an innocent country girl leaves her home suddenly it is a good rule to look for—the man."

"You think some one lured Elsie away?" said Patience stifled by the thought. "That some man is to blame?"

"It isn't an easy thing to say, my dear, but I do."

"Aren't there laws against such crimes?"

"Yes," replied Miss Masters, "but these laws were made by men, and men have always shown an unwillingness to legislate against their sex. Now there were some young men in Millville at the time your sister went away, weren't there?"

"Yes," admitted Patience, "two."

"Do you know their names?"

"Martin Druce."

"Ah!"

"You know him?"

"I have seen him." Miss Masters opened her memorandum book. "Martin Druce," she read, "dealer in live stock."

"Yes," assented Patience, "he told us that was his business."

"And the other stranger, Miss Welcome? Do not hide any of the facts."

"I'd rather not say," replied Patience hesitatingly.

"You had better tell me," urged Miss Masters.

"I—I can't," exclaimed the girl, "it hurts me even to think that he—"

"Better tell me," Miss Masters persisted.

"The other young man," said Patience, "was—Harry Boland."

"What?" exclaimed Miss Masters sharply.

"You know Harry Boland?" Patience flushed and stood up.

"I do. You are in the Bolands' outer offices at this moment."

She had scarcely spoken when the door of Harry Boland's office opened and the young man came out.

Patience drew her heavy veil down over her face and darted toward the outer door.

"Here is a corrected form of that contract, Miss Masters," said young Boland brusquely.

CHAPTER XVI

JOHN BOLAND MEETS MARY RANDALL

But Patience did not leave the office of the Lake City Electrical Company as quickly as she had hoped to do. She was intercepted by the young man, who deliberately placed himself between her and the door, effectually blocking the way.

He eyed the small figure in black with an inquisitiveness which was almost rude, attempting to peer through the meshes of the heavy veil, as he spoke to Miss Masters:

"I beg your pardon, I thought you were alone."

Before she could reply a rasping voice called from the inner office:

"Oh, Harry, send Miss Masters in here, will you?"

"The Governor wants you, Miss Masters," said Harry, his eyes still on Patience.

"I'm coming, Mr. Boland," proclaimed the stenographer.

With only a glance at her companions, she made a detour of

the desk in the center of the room and glided into the other office.

"I'm afraid Miss Masters may be kept busy for some time," volunteered Harry kindly, "but if—if you care to wait—"

Patience only bowed her head and attempted to pass him; but she caught her breath quickly and her body swayed slightly, but perceptibly.

"I beg your pardon," went on Harry, fencing for time.

Again endeavoring to pass him, she staggered and put out one hand to steady herself, which Harry clasped quickly.

"Let me help you," he said.

She made a movement to release her hand as she recovered from the dizziness which had seized her.

"Better put up your veil, dear," said Harry gently. "I'm sure it is you."

"Please!" pleaded Patience. The word was scarcely audible.

"Put up your veil," he persisted.

When she complied, he gazed into her deep, dark eyes and stroked her hand tenderly.

"Did you think I could be in the same room with you and not know you? Oh, my dear—"

"No, Harry, no!" protested Patience, withdrawing her hand.

"If you knew how long and patiently I've searched for you, I don't think you could be so unkind."

"It's the only safe way," she replied, stepping away from him and clutching the back of a chair.

"Why?" he asked as he went close to her again.

"Because—because—"

"Because you do really care for me and you're fighting against yourself."

"Please let me go," begged Patience.

"No!" returned the young man stoutly.

"What shall I do?" she pleaded distractedly.

"Just turn around," was the smiling retort, "and run straight into the arms of the man who loves you."

"And bring trouble and sorrow on you? No—no—no!"

"I don't understand."

"Please don't ask me," she went on. "I've been through the deep waters of grief and suffering. Harry, I've been hungry."

"Hungry!" exclaimed Harry. "Oh, my poor girl, you must let me—"

Patience shook her head slowly, sadly; an eager light of desire for his love and tender care illuminated her face.

"Do you love me?" pursued the young man fervently.

"You mustn't ask me that—wait!"

"And lose you again?" He laid his hand on one of hers. "No; I want my answer now."

A harsh, commanding voice interrupted them.

"Harry!"

Patience started and drew her hand from beneath the other's touch as an elderly man came into the room.

"Governor!" exclaimed Harry, a little surprised, but entirely composed as he went on:

"Governor, I want you to meet the young lady who is to be my wife."

"What!" ejaculated John Boland, scarcely believing his own ears.

"Miss Patience Welcome."

"Welcome?" the older man turned his back to conceal the startled expression which came over his features.

"Yes. This is my good old dad, Patience," said Harry, laying one arm affectionately about his father's shoulders.

"Rather sudden, isn't it?" demanded Boland, senior, in a sharp tone.

But Harry was accustomed to his father's abrupt ways and gave no heed to the testiness of the query.

"No, Governor, I met Miss Welcome when I was in Millville."

"Oh, yes," hemmed John Boland, truculently unmindful of the introduction. "But just now get that contract off; Miss Masters is waiting."

"All right," assented Harry cheerfully. Then he turned to Patience. "I won't be long, dear."

Boland placed himself before his desk, covertly watching from beneath his shaggy, lowered brows until his son had disappeared. Then he cleared his throat and wheeled upon Patience without ceremony.

"Now, listen, Miss Welcome, you're not taking this seriously, I hope."

"No, Mr. Boland," she replied, moving toward the door. "I've tried to tell Harry how impossible it is—that—"

"You're a sensible girl," he broke in bluntly. "As it happens, Harry is already engaged."

The girl's breath came in short, sharp gasps, but she managed to control her voice as she murmured:

"He is?"

"Yes."

Boland placed his fingers in his vest pocket and drew out a fountain pen, the point of which he examined attentively. Patience felt that she ought to go at once, but somehow she couldn't. She stood there trembling, scarcely knowing whether or not she should believe the other's statement. She could not believe that Harry would do such an ignoble thing.

Boland glanced over his shoulder and saw her still hesitating on the threshold.

"Yes," he repeated blandly. "He is going to marry the daughter of my business partner—a girl who will inherit half a million."

He could see from the corner of his eye that the shot had told, but still Patience lingered, dazed.

"I—I see," she faltered weakly.

"Now you go along like a good girl," advised Boland, "and I'll see that you are treated fairly."

He opened a pretentious looking check book which lay on the desk.

"Just tell me how much you want and—"

"Nothing!" was the firm, decisive reply.

He eyed the girl critically as he remarked:

"You look as though ready money were a stranger to you."

"It is—but I have a position with the Mining Company in this building."

"I know them," declared Boland thoughtfully. Patience made no comment. She went on proudly, drawing her figure to its full height:

"And I want nothing; I am *giving* you back your son, Mr. Boland, I am not selling him to you."

He shrugged his shoulders and stared stupidly at the vacant

doorway as he heard the girlish voice in the hallway, saying:

"Down, please."

He closed his check book with a snap, and involuntarily fumbled about his well arranged desk, replacing a paper here and a contract there.

"Hum!" he mused, "I thought there was something wrong with Harry."

The desk telephone rang sharply. He picked up the instrument and placed the receiver to his ear.

"Hello! hello!" he jerked out irritably. "Yes—yes, this is John Boland. Who wants me?"

His acute features contracted as he listened to the reply.

"Oh, Martin Druce," he said. "Want to see me about the lease of the Cafe Sinister, eh?"

His mind worked rapidly while he again listened.

"All right," he blustered finally, "all right, see you in fifteen minutes. Yes,—yes, here!"

He hung up the receiver and took a cigar from his pocket, thoughtfully biting off the end, as he muttered half aloud:

"Martin Druce, eh? Cafe Sinister—Ah!"

His lips ceased moving as he looked about him. He was still thinking deeply; then he struck a match and lighted the cigar at the glowing flame which he contemplated for a second before extinguishing it. With a look of one who has just solved a problem, he cast aside the charred ember and gritted:

"I guess so."

He seized a sheet of paper and rapidly scratched a few words on its white surface, settling back comfortably in the big chair as Harry came in.

"All right, Governor," called out the son; but he paused in astonishment when he saw that his father was alone. "Why— why, where's Patience?"

"Miss Welcome had to go,—she said," returned the other, calmly puffing his cigar.

"Didn't she leave any word for me?"

"Yes, she said she'd see you again."

"When?" asked Harry, impatiently. "Why, I don't even know where she lives."

"I thought of that," replied his father, as he handed the memorandum slip to Harry, on which he had just written. "Here's her address."

Harry took the bit of paper gratefully, and looked at it.

"Why—"

"What's the matter?" John Boland surveyed the wrapper of his cigar with keen interest, deftly closing a small broken place in it.

"This address!" exclaimed Harry.

"Well, what about it?"

"It's in the lowest, most depraved section of the city."

"Yes, I noticed that."

Harry looked up at his father quizzically.

"You did?"

"Yes."

"Governor," began Harry pointedly, a new idea beginning to dawn upon him, "if you do not know that a great deal of your property is rented and used for the most immoral purposes how do you know this address so well?"

"Why," spluttered Boland, senior, "I—I've read the papers."

"But this vile section of the city that you own has never been published."

"Look here, Harry," demanded his father, aggressively, "do you doubt my word?"

"I do," was the firm reply.

"I'm your father," he retorted angrily.

"You are," agreed Harry, "but this is a matter of right and wrong, and you can't fool me again as you have all these years."

"I'll show you who's master," threatened John Boland, grimly.

"It's your privilege to try," conceded the son with suppressed anger.

"Hold on—hold on," hedged his father, apologetically, "don't let's get mad about it. Finish up that contract and then—"

"And then?"

Harry's manner was alert, defensive, but wholly questioning.

"Then we'll talk this over calmly."

"All right, but Governor—" the young man turned at the door, grasping the contract in one hand as he put out the other warningly and pointed with his forefinger to the scrap of paper he had laid on the desk, on which was written Patience's supposed address: "Let me give you a piece of advice. Don't try to fool me."

John Boland stood motionless for a moment looking after his son; then he clenched his hand and brought it down on the desk with a forcible thump, as he thought:

"I've got to do something—quick."

"Well, made up your mind to see me, did you, Mr. Boland?"

Martin Druce's suave voice recalled Boland from the revery into which he had lapsed.

"Yes," he replied quickly, walking to the door through which Harry had gone and closing it.

"Now, don't talk," he commanded as he returned to his desk. "Listen! You and Anson want a renewal of the lease for the Cafe Sinister, don't you?"

"Sure," responded Druce, affably. "And I suppose you'll raise the rent on us."

"No," replied Boland, shaking his head.

"Eh?"

"Not if you're smart."

"I don't get you," announced Druce inquiringly, as he seated himself on the edge of the desk.

"My boy, Harry, thinks he is in love with a girl who has come to Chicago."

"Yes, Mr. Boland, but I don't see—"

"Now," continued Boland, regardless of the interruption, "if Harry happened to see this girl in some questionable resort, —say, like Cafe Sinister—if he were tipped off that this girl would be there—"

"I get you." Druce sprang to his feet; he was now keen and alert, like a hound on the scent. "Who's the girl?"

"She's got a position of some kind with the Alpha Mining Company on this floor," replied Boland. "She'll lose that tomorrow."

"I'm on. What's her name?"

"Patience Welcome!"

"What!" exclaimed Druce, with a sneering twist to the word.

"Do you know her?"

"Yes."

"Well?" Boland gazed at him, anxiously awaiting the reply.

"About the lease?" veered Druce with cunning perception.

Boland hesitated and scrutinized the other closely. He was satisfied with what he saw stamped on Druce's face, but he only said pointedly:

"I always make good when a man delivers the goods. Now get out—I'm busy."

"On my way," returned Druce easily, as he sauntered to the door, but he turned there, saying significantly:

"I'll deliver the goods,—don't worry."

John Boland sighed contentedly as he watched Druce go. Then he muttered:

"There, I guess I—"

"All right, Mr. Boland," rang out a clear feminine voice, as Miss Masters came from the inner office. "That contract is all ready."

"Oh, Miss Masters!"

"Yes, Mr. Boland," she replied in saccharine tones.

"Make out a lease for that property in South Twelfth street."

"For the Cafe Sinister, John?" inquired Michael Grogan, who had followed Miss Masters into the main office. "You're crazy."

"Oh, shut up, Mike," snapped Boland. "What ails you, anyway?"

"I've been reading the last edition," replied Grogan, lugubriously. "Mary Randall has had special officers sworn in at her own expense to help her make raids. She's put goose flesh all over me."

"Let me see it."

Boland took the paper which Grogan was fingering nervously.

"Take it," said the Irishman. "It's a live coal."

The other glanced over the sheet and threw it on the desk.

"Get busy on that lease, Miss Masters," he commanded.

"Just a moment, Governor," interrupted Harry, who had overheard the conversation as he came in. "If you lease that property to that hound, Anson, you and I are through."

"What?" exclaimed John Boland, astounded.

"It has come to a show-down," went on Harry, with determination expressed in both his tone and manner, "and I'm damned if I'll touch a cent of dirty money like that."

"You've been reading the Mary Randall stuff, eh?" sneered his father.

"Yes. And she's right. Now, you make your choice."

"Hold on—hold on," commanded the irate father. "Aren't you forgetting that I own and control this Lake City

Company—that you are—"

"No! I realize that," retorted Harry, resolutely.

"All right!" Boland turned to Miss Masters grimly: "Make out that lease to Anson."

"Then here," said Harry quietly, as he wrote a few words on a sheet of blank paper and laid it on the desk; "here is my resignation as president of your Electrical Company, to take effect *now*."

"Harry!" protested his father.

"I'll get my personal things together at once," went on the young man, securing his hat from the rack.

"This has gone far enough," rasped John Boland, springing to his feet. "I'll show this Mary Randall there's one she can't scare."

He paced nervously up and down the office, pausing finally beside his desk.

"Miss Masters, take an open letter from me to the newspapers."

He did not notice the actions of the stenographer as he dictated:

"I, John Boland, am a business man. I stand on my record. I defy Miss Mary Randall—"

In pausing to formulate his thoughts, he became conscious that Miss Masters had not been taking his dictation; that she had laid an envelope on his desk directly in front of where he usually sat, and that she was putting on her hat.

"Here, hold on!" he cried peremptorily. "What does this mean, Miss Masters?"

"It means, Mr. Boland," she replied quietly, as she adjusted a hat pin, "that I have resigned. Good day."

When she started to leave Boland called out to her in amazement:

"Here—wait—why do you resign?"

"That letter on the desk will tell you," she said as she moved through the doorway. "Good day."

John Boland picked up the letter and opened it. He was dazed as he read aloud:

"I refuse to lend my aid to the owners of vice property. Mary Randall."

Boland stared into space, while Harry exclaimed:

"Then Miss Masters is Mary Randall!"

"Murder, alive!" yelled Grogan. He slid down in his chair and attempted to conceal himself beneath the desk.

John Boland's hands trembled as he clutched the letter.

"Mary Randall," he said, still dazed. "By all that's holy! That girl Mary Randall!"

CHAPTER XVII

THE CAFE SINISTER

The Cafe Sinister stands like a gilded temple at the entrance to Chicago's tenderloin. The fact is significant. The management, the appearance, the policy, if you please, of the place are all in keeping with this one potent circumstance of location. The Cafe Sinister beckons to the passerby. It appeals to him subtly with its music, its cheap splendor, its false gayety. To the sophisticated its allurements are those of the scarlet woman, to the innocent its voice is the voice of Joy.

Two pillars of carved glass, lighted from the inside by electricity, stand at the portal. Within a huge room, filled with drinking tables sparkling with many lights, gleaming and garish, suggests without revealing the enticements of evil.

This is the set trap. Above is that indispensable appurtenance to the pander's trade—the private dining room. Above that is what, in the infinite courtesy of the police, is called a hotel. And behind and beyond lies the Levee itself—naked and unashamed, blatantly vicious, consuming itself in the caustic of its own vices.

To the trained observer of cities the words: "All hope abandon, ye who enter here," are written as plainly over the door of the Cafe Sinister as if it were that other portal through which Dante passed with Beatrice. But the unlearned in vice cannot read the writing. By thousands every year they enter joyously and by thousands they are cast out into the Levee, wrecked in morals, ruined in health, racked by their own consciences.

The Cafe Sinister is not an institution peculiar to Chicago. Every great city in America possesses one. It is the place through which recruits are won to the underworld. It is the entrance to the labyrinth where lost souls wander. Viewed from its portal it is the Palace of Pleasure; seen from behind, through those haggard eyes from which vice has torn away the illusions of innocence, it is the Saddest Place in the World.

Druce owned the Cafe Sinister with Carter Anson; their lease was written for them by John Boland. Thus the upper world and the under were leagued for its maintenance. And though the press might shriek and the pulpit thunder the combination and the Cafe Sinister went on forever.

These three men had been drawn together by a common characteristic. Their consciences were dead. That atrophy of conscience made them all worshipers of the same idol— money. The motives that propelled each of the three to the altar were as diverse as their separate natures, but the sacrifice that each offered to the Moloch was the same— their souls.

Having forfeited by their deeds the thing that made them men, the three shrunk to the moral stature of animals. Boland was the tiger, brooding over the city with yellow eyes, seeking whom he might devour. Druce was the wolf;

cunning, ruthless, prowling. Anson was the mastiff; savage, brutal, given to wild bursts of rending passion. Love of power lashed Boland to his crimes; lechery prompted Druce in his prowlings; and whisky was the fire that smouldered under Anson's brutalities.

On an afternoon in June Druce and Anson sat together in conference in one of the little booths of the Cafe Sinister's main dining room. The cafe, after its orgy of the night before, was quiet. Waiters, cat-footed and villain faced, gathered up the debris of the night's revel, slinking about their work like men ashamed of it. The sunlight peered dimly through the curtained windows; the air was heavy with the lees of liquor and the dead smoke of tobacco.

The two men sat facing each other. A glass of whisky was cupped in Anson's closed hand. His clothes, unbrushed and unpressed, flapped about his huge figure. His throat bagged with flabby dewlaps. His head was bullet-shaped, his eyes fierce, his mouth loose-lipped and brutal. He made a strange contrast to his companion. Druce was lithe, well made and gifted with a sort of Satanic handsomeness. He was immaculately dressed.

"It's fixed, I tell you," Druce was saying.

"Fixed, be damned," rumbled Anson. "I know Boland. Nothing's fixed with him until the lease is drawn and delivered."

"I say the thing's fixed," insisted Druce. "All we've got to do now is carry out our part of the agreement and I've completed all of the arrangements. We've got a week."

"I know," said Anson, unconvinced. "It's fixed and you've completed the arrangements. I'm from Missouri."

"Boland wants this girl, Patience Welcome, brought in here next Saturday night," said Druce. "He has arranged that his pious pup of a son, Harry, shall be here the same evening. We are to manage it so that he will get the impression that the girl has been amusing herself with him, that she has been kidding him along and playing this tenderloin game on the side. He's not to be allowed to talk to her. He'll see her—that will be enough. She's to come here to help her mother earn a little cash. I sent a fellow to hire the old woman to start here on Saturday night as a scrub woman. She's agreed to keep that part of it quiet. Then I'll drag the other one in—mine, do you understand. We'll make young Boland think the whole damned Welcome family belongs to us. We can see to it that the Patience girl gets some glad rags and some dope when she gets here. She's seen me in Millville, so it's up to you, Anson, to sign her up at good pay as a singer—" He stopped significantly.

"Too complicated," was Anson's rejoinder. "Sounds good on paper, but it won't work, I tell you, it won't work. I don't like the way things have been going lately." He drained the whisky glass. "This vice commission and this crazy yap of a Mary Randall—"

"O, hell!" interrupted Druce in disgust. "You've got it, too, have you? Mary Randall! My God, you talk like an old woman!"

"I tell you—" Anson began.

"You can't tell me nothing. I'm sick and tired of framing stuff and then have you throw it down because you've lost your nerve and are afraid of a girl. I'm done, I tell you. If you think you can improve on my plans, go ahead. I'm through. I won't—"

Anson capitulated immediately. "Now don't get sore, Mart," he whined, "I know I'm no good on this frameup stuff. Maybe I am a little nervous. Go ahead with your plan—I guess it's the best one. Don't let's fight about it."

"All right," rejoined Druce. "Now that's settled. I'll handle this thing. All you've got to do is keep your trap shut and stand pat."

The conversation was interrupted by the angry and maudlin exclamations of a girl. She had been sitting at a distant table half asleep. A porter had wakened her.

"I won't go home and sleep," she shrieked. "Keep your hands off me, you dirty nigger."

"Now what's the trouble?" demanded Druce of Anson.

"Swede Rose has been drunk all night."

"We've got to get rid of her. She's always pulling this rough stuff."

"Not now," warned Anson. "It's too hard to get new girls. When she's sober she's a wise money getter."

"Damn her," muttered Druce, "I don't like her anyway. She had the nerve to slap my face the other night because I wouldn't give her money for hop. As soon as this lease is signed I'm going down state. I'll bring back some new stock and then it's 'On your way' for that wildcat."

"Let me handle her," advised Anson. He got up and walked over to the table where the girl was having the altercation with the negro. She was still young, but drink and drugs had left ineffaceable lines upon her face. She was beautiful, even this morning after her night's debauch, for she possessed a regularity of feature and a fine contour of figure that not even death itself could wreck. Her disheveled hair showed here and there traces of gray. Her skin was a dead white, save where two pink spots blazed in either cheek.

"Here he comes," called the girl, catching sight of Anson. "Good old Carter. Ans," she went on, "chase this coon out of here; he won't let me sleep." Anson motioned the porter to keep his distance. "An' say, Ans," the girl went on, "gimme a quarter. I'm broke and I got to have some hop or die."

Anson handed the negro a quarter without a word. The porter hurried out of the cafe.

"He wanted to chase me out," the girl whimpered.

"Well, Rose," Anson went on pacifically, "you've got to cut out this all night booze thing. You're hurting the house."

The girl looked up at the dive keeper with dull eyes.

"Hurting the house, eh?" she echoed. "What about me? Think I ain't hurting myself? Say, it's got so I'd rather be drunk than sober. I can't stand to be sober. I always start thinking. Some of these days you'll hear of me walking out of this place and making a dent in the lake—"

The negro returned with the drug. The girl seized it with trembling hands. While the two men stood and looked she drew a small lancet from the bosom of her dress, inserted its point under the skin of her white forearm and drove a few drops of the drug into the vein. The effect was instantaneous. She laughed loudly.

"Now, you get to bed," ordered Anson.

"Bed, hell," retorted the girl.

"I said get to bed." Anson glowered at her.

"There'll be a big night tonight, and—"

"You can't give me no orders."

Anson had held in his temper as long as he was able. His fierce eyes twinkled and his brutal mouth twitched. Without a word he reached across the table, clutched the girl by the throat and dragged her out of her seat. He hurled her, half strangled, on the floor.

"Here," he bellowed to some of his servitors, "take this damn hell-cat out of here. Take her up to the hotel. If she won't go to bed, throw her into the street."

"You—you—" gasped the girl, struggling to her feet.

"Don't talk back to me," roared Anson, "or I'll kill you. I'll show you what you are and who's running this place." Then to the waiters: "Get her out of here."

The girl was dragged out of the room, screaming and fighting. A wisp of curses came back into the big room as she was lugged up the stairs towards the hotel.

Anson stood panting with anger. A mail carrier entered and placed a letter in his hand. He opened and read:

"Mr. Carter Anson: Take your choice. Close the Cafe Sinister, or I'll see that it is closed. Mary Randall."

The big man flushed crimson with rage. He tried to speak, but the words choked in his throat. He crumpled the letter and hurled it with a curse across the room.

"Druce," he bellowed.

Druce hurried across the room.

"Did you see that?"

"Yes, I saw you beat her up. Why don't you let 'em alone? You'll kill one of them some of these days."

"Naw, not her. I mean the letter. Mary Randall—she says she's going to close us." A waiter recovered the letter and brought it to Druce. He read it.

"Say, listen, are you turning yellow—"

"No, I ain't yellow," returned Anson, "but this thing is getting my goat. You're sure about that lease?"

"Sure?—say, I thought we'd settled that—"

"Well," pursued Anson, "I don't like this. What have you done with this other girl—the one you married? She'll be getting us into a row next."

"I married her, didn't I?"

"Yes, but—"

"Well, it's about time she started earning her bread. This Randall woman hasn't got me scared. You know why I married her. Well, I'm going through with it. I—"

The rest of his sentence died on his lips. A girl scarcely more than a child came in from the hotel entrance. She was dressed in a lacey gown, a size too large for her. The slit skirt displayed her slim ankles in pink silk stockings. The French heeled shoes were decorated with rhinestone buckles. In spite of this outrageous dress she was still pretty. It was Elsie Welcome.

"Hello, kid," said Druce, his manner changing.

"I want to see you, Martin," Elsie replied. Druce noticed that she seemed deeply agitated. There were signs of recently shed tears on her cheeks.

"I'll run along," said Anson, seeing the girl's agitation. When he was gone Druce drew the girl into a booth and demanded sharply:

"What the devil do you want and how did you get here?"

"I came in a taxicab," the girl answered.

"A taxi, eh? Well, you're learning. Who paid for it?"

"It isn't paid for, Martin. I wanted to see you and—"

"And what?"

"The man's waiting outside."

Druce flushed angrily. "Look here," he demanded. "Don't play me for a boob. Get someone else to pay your taxi bills."

"But, Martin, I thought—"

Druce did not wait for the rest of the sentence. With a muttered oath he rushed outside and paid the waiting chauffeur.

"Now, what do you want?" he demanded when he returned.

Elsie looked at him piteously. "Martin," she said, "I can't stay in that place any longer."

"Say, don't my aunt treat you all right?"

The girl burst out sobbing. "She isn't your aunt, Martin. She told me so herself. And that flat—"

"Well, what about it?"

"I—I can't tell you. I can't say it. I never knew until tonight." Elsie clutched Druce's arm pleadingly. "Martin," she said, "a man came into my room."

Druce saw that the time had come for him to lay his cards on the table. He folded his arms and looked at the girl.

"Well?" he demanded coolly.

"He had been drinking and—he took hold of me."

There was a long pause. Druce gazed at the girl satirically. She quailed with sinking heart under that look. She began sobbing again.

"Don't look at me like that, Martin," she wailed. "Don't—or I shall go mad. I left home to marry you."

"Well, I married you, didn't I?" Druce sneered.

Elsie attempted to control her voice.

"That woman you call your aunt laughed at me when I told her I was your wife. She said I was a country fool."

"Damn her," muttered Druce. "I'll settle with her."

The girl grasped Druce frantically.

"Tell me she lied," she cried, "or I'll go crazy. Tell me she lied."

"Yes, she lied," answered Druce glibly. "See here, kid, it's about time you began helping to support the family."

Elsie dried her tears. "I'm—I'm ready," she said. "I've practiced my songs—"

"O, the songs," said Druce. "That isn't all."

"What do you mean, Martin?"

"Why—don't be so stand-offish. When a man offers to buy you a bottle of wine, let him."

"Martin!"

Druce stopped her sharply. "Now don't begin that Millville Sunday school stuff," he said. "This is business."

"Is it?" Elsie spoke in a whisper.

"Sure. When a man's got a wad of bills and he's willing to buy, string him along!"

"But I'm your wife, Martin." Elsie was dead white and calm.

"Well, don't let that worry you. Go as far as you like—or as far as he likes."

The girl stood motionless, looking straight before her.

Virginia Brooks

"Is—is that what you brought me here for?" she asked with forced calmness.

"Sure. Why do you suppose I dressed you up like that? Your stock in trade is your good looks. Sell it."

The girl drew herself up rigidly.

"I won't do it," she said. She started toward the door.

"You will!" grated Druce, following her.

"Never," she answered. "I'll die first. Good-by!" The door closed after her.

Anson had returned to the room and had witnessed the scene.

"Well," he sneered, "there goes the first move in your plan. You've lost that one."

"You think so?" Druce sneered in return. "Well, don't lose any sleep worrying about that one. She ain't got a dime. She'll be back."

CHAPTER XVIII

LOST IN THE LEVEE

So stupefied was Elsie Welcome by her emotions as she fled from the Cafe Sinister that it was not until her clothes were drenched that she realized it had begun to rain. Even then she did not halt and seek shelter. Her numbed brain knew only one thing—that she must get away from Druce and the place of sin to which he had brought her.

Up to the time of her last interview with her husband she had been living in a dream; now that dream had turned into a nightmare. But the nightmare, she at last realized, was reality. The veil of deception Druce had woven around her had been torn away by his own brutal words. She had come to feel a vague terror of the man. As for the Cafe Sinister, her whole nature revolted against it.

It was an hour before sunset. The sullen houses about her were beginning to show signs of life. Here and there a door opened and a man or woman stepped quickly out with rapid glances up and down the street. There was no loitering. They went their way quickly, always with a half furtive look over the shoulder.

As the girl reached a corner she found at last that she was too exhausted to go farther. Her clothes dripped. She sought an entrance way for shelter. A tall girl in a broad hat with showy plumes was just coming out of the door. She looked at Elsie's tear stained face and stopped.

"What's the matter, girlie?" There was sympathy in her voice.

"Nothing. Can you tell me where this number is?" She produced a card on which Druce's "aunt" at their last interview had written the address of a woman from whom she could get work.

The tall girl glanced at the slip of paper.

"It's just over there, two doors from that corner," she said. Elsie turned to cross the street. The tall girl stood still regarding her thoughtfully. Suddenly she seemed to reach a decision. She darted forward and stopped Elsie.

"It's none of my business, kid," she said, "but what do you want of Mother Lankee?"

Elsie looked at her in surprise. "Why," she said pitifully, "I expect to get work there."

"Do you know the kind of work Mother Lankee would ask you to do?"

"I don't know, but I'm willing to do anything."

"Anything?" repeated the tall girl.

"Why, yes. I've got to the point where I can't afford to be particular."

The tall girl laid her hand on Elsie's arm.

"What is your name?"

"Elsie Welcome."

"Where do you live?"

"On South Tenth street."

"You come from down state?"

"How did you know?"

"It's written all over you. What man brought you here?"

The question surprised Elsie and brought back memory of her sorrows. She did not answer. Her eyes filled with tears.

"Come, kid," said the tall girl, cheerfully, "get hold of your-self. Now, listen! You stay away from Mother Lankee. You're hungry, ain't you, dearie? You come with me and we'll get something to eat."

Elsie was too tired to resist and, instinctively, she trusted this tall girl with her assumption of guardianship. Together they crossed the street and entered the rear room of a saloon. Three men sat near the entrance playing cards. They looked at the two girls, inspecting Elsie narrowly and nodding carelessly at her companion. The girl took seats at a distant table.

"What do you want, Lou?" inquired one of the men, getting up from the table.

"Not you," retorted Lou curtly. "Send one of your waiters

here with a plain lemonade, a glass of milk and some of that beef stew."

"Milk, eh?" said the man, "and lemonade. On the wagon again, Lou?"

"Run along now," returned the girl. "If you keep on asking questions someone is going to tell you lies."

The man went into another room, spoke to someone there and rejoined the card players. In a few moments a negro waiter appeared with the viands Lou had ordered.

Elsie began to eat famishedly. The other girl watched her approvingly.

"Go to it, girlie," she advised. "I know how you feel. I've been hungry myself."

She sipped her lemonade until Elsie had finished. Then, as though it had not been interrupted, she resumed the conversation they had begun in the street.

"The same old game," she said cynically. "You came to Chicago because you loved him. He strung you along—" Her glance fell on Elsie's wedding ring. "You fell for that 'I do take thee' thing. Then he shook you. Is that right, girlie?"

Elsie shook her head. A stupor due to the food and the reaction from her nervous and physical exhaustion came over her. She felt too languid to grapple with the problem of existence.

The tall girl arched her eyebrows in surprise.

"He didn't shake you? Then why—"

"I couldn't do what he wanted me to do," murmured Elsie. She felt her face flushing and she dropped her head. "He wanted me to—to—"

The other interrupted her sharply. "You needn't say it—I know." She gripped the table in sudden anger. "One of these dogs—eh?"

Elsie stared at her blankly. The old sense of forlornness, of being alone and uncared for, returned to her.

"I don't know what you mean," she faltered.

"What was his name?"

"Druce," gasped Elsie.

"Druce, eh?" replied the tall girl, as though the name had opened a whole vista of understanding. "Druce? Well, look out for him, girlie. He'll hound you from one end of the town to the other until he gets you. That's his business."

"He always said he was a dealer in live stock."

The tall girl laughed scornfully. "Live stock!" she jeered. "Did he get away with that? Well, that's what he is—a dealer in human live stock, a trafficker in women, one of the oldest professions in the world—and the dirtiest. Live stock! That's what he calls girls like you and me—cattle!"

For a long moment Elsie sat staring at her companion. The last prop of her faith in the man who had married her was crumbling. She could not give up this last illusion of Druce's faithfulness without a struggle. The blood flamed to her cheeks and she started to her feet.

"I don't believe it," she cried in anguish.

To her surprise, Lou made no reply. She merely regarded her pityingly. This was the last blow. Elsie burst into a flood of tears.

"I know you don't believe it," said Lou gently. "It's hard for anyone who is decent to believe that men can fall so low. Why, nobody believes it! The men who run the city government don't believe it, the law makers don't believe it, the vice commission, doesn't believe it. The only people who believe it are the people who, at their own bitter cost, know it—and this girl Mary Randall."

She paused.

"Look at me, kid," she went on. "I was sold for $175. Sold, do you get that? SOLD! And I came high. They buy and sell 'em in this district every day for fifty. Yes, I was prime stock. They brought me up here from Kentucky. Kentucky Lou, price $175—a choice article." She broke off, laughing bitterly, and summoned a waiter.

"Whisky," she said, "and be quick with it."

She waited until the waiter returned without speaking. Then she tossed off the glass of fiery liquid like a man.

"Now," she said, resuming the conversation abruptly, "let me tell you what you are up against. You can't go home, your pride won't let you. And if you wanted to go home you haven't the money. Druce has turned you loose in this district to starve and when you've starved enough you'll come back to him."

Elsie shook her head.

"Yes, you will, girlie. You don't know it now, but I know it and Druce knows it. And when you come back you'll do as Druce wants you to do, because you'll know that if you don't you'll have to starve again. It's against human nature to starve. You'll go back to him. And when you do and Druce is tired of you he'll sell you for what you are, cattle—his kind of cattle!"

"Oh no!" wailed Elsie. "Not that. Surely in this great city there are places where a friendless girl can find protection!"

Kentucky Lou laughed again but the laugh contained no mirth.

"I thought that too, kid," she said more gently. "And perhaps —perhaps—if you could find the right people and they believed you they might help you. But they didn't help me. I went to one of these institutions that advertise to help friendless girls. Yes, I went to them. I had my baby in my arms. And they began by shooting me full of questions that I'd rather die than answer. And me perishing for a kind word and a slap on the back—just something to keep me fighting to be good. They gave me tracts, and sermons and advice. And then my baby died and I didn't care what happened. I guess I went crazy after that. 'It's hell, anyway,' I says, 'so here goes.' And here I am."

While she spoke Kentucky Lou was fumbling with her dress. Her hand reappeared in a moment with a five dollar bill. She shoved the bill into Elsie's hand.

"Take that," she said, "and go. Go as far as you can. It's all I can do for you and it may save you. I think you'll come back to Druce but I'm taking a gambler's chance."

She took Elsie by the arm, half lifted the stupefied girl to her feet and led her to the door. Impelled by a terror which both blinded and choked her Elsie fled into the gathering darkness without even pausing to thank her benefactor.

Lou returned to the saloon and ordered more whisky.

"Lou," inquired one of the men, "who's you're friend?"

Lou regarded the questioner calmly.

"That?" she replied, "Oh, that's a little lost lamb turned loose in a den of you human hyenas."

CHAPTER XIX

MARY RANDALL GOES TO LIVE IN A WOLF'S DEN

Martin Druce, still pacing uneasily; about the big drinking room of the Cafe Sinister after his angry parting with Elsie Welcome, looked up suddenly and saw the street door open. He stood still staring. The new arrival was Mary Randall. She wore a smart tailored suit and a modish hat. Druce noted these details of costume, the shining bronze hair, the fresh complexion and the trim figure. He gasped with surprise.

Druce's surprise was not due to any recognition of his visitor as the reformer. To him Mary Randall was still Miss Masters, for he had heard nothing of the episode in John Boland's office when the electric king's private secretary revealed her true identity. His astonishment was predicated upon the fact that this stenographer, after having thwarted and flouted him, after having seemed to read the darkest secrets of his plotting mind, should now walk in upon him with all the easy composure of an old friend.

Then he had read the girl wrong after all! She was, as he had at first suspected, of the demi-monde. Thus her sophistication, the ease with which she had penetrated his pretensions, the cool finality with which she had catalogued and placed him, were all explainable. Her worldly wisdom, which he had found so baffling, was that of the skilled and experienced adventuress!

These reflections swept through his mind in a moment. Another thought came to him that filled him with rage. She was here now to resume her play with him. But rage gave way to desire. His mind instantly busied itself with new intrigues. Here was a woman much to be desired. She had come hunting amusement at his expense. She delivered herself into his hands; she laughed at his power. And she seemed confident of beating him. This was a game that filled him with delight. He sprang forward eagerly to greet her, bowing gallantly, and doffing his hat.

"How do you do, Mr. Druce?" inquired Miss Masters. "You seem surprised to see me here."

Druce caught something mocking in her tone. "I'm more than surprised," he returned. "I'm tickled pink. Won't you have a seat?" He prepared a place for her at one of the booths. "And can't I order you something to drink?"

Miss Masters favored Druce with one of her enigmatical smiles. "It's a little early for wine," she said, "and too late for highballs. Besides, business before pleasure. I want to talk to you."

Druce sat down, expectantly.

"I've come here, Mr. Druce," Miss Masters went on, "not merely to make a social call, as you seem to take for granted, but as John Boland's agent. He has instructed me to take up the matter of your new lease with you. I am to handle the whole transaction in his name. The only stipulation that he makes is that you are not to communicate with him again. He wants you to stay away from his office, because he has learned within the last few hours that the office is being watched by agents of this girl reformer, Mary Randall. He has instructed me to tell you not to attempt to see him or to telephone him until your negotiations with me are concluded."

Druce was disappointed.

"Why," he said, "I thought the matter of the lease was settled. Boland told me plainly when I last talked with him that if I would arrange to have Patience Welcome here on Saturday night so that Harry Boland could see her he would give me a new lease with no increase in rental."

"I understand," replied Miss Masters to whom this was news. "The idea of arranging this meeting is, I am informed, to convince Harry that the girl has been playing with him—that she is one of your employes."

"That's it," replied Druce. "I've made all the plans and the girl will be here on Saturday night. I've arranged to have her mother here, too. And to make it good I expect to bring in the other sister—the girl Elsie—at the last moment. Young Boland will believe that the whole Welcome family is working for me."

"I see," said Miss Masters. "It's a pretty smooth scheme, but Mr. Boland thinks it's rather too daring. That's why he's sent me here, to see that nothing goes wrong. You are to give me all the details of your plans and through me Mr. Boland is to be kept informed as to what is going on."

"Well, he's a deep one," said Druce. "I don't like his introducing a third party into my plans very well, but I guess I've got to take it. I've got to have that lease."

"Yes," replied Miss Masters, "that's the way John Boland has it figured out."

"Say, girlie," Druce went on, assuming a confidential air, "Old Boland sure must have a lot of confidence in you."

Again Miss Masters smiled enigmatically. "Yes," she admitted, "Mr. Boland has reason to know I can take care of myself in nearly every situation."

"I'm beginning to think you're as deep as Boland is."

"Yes?" Miss Masters tantalized him with another of her smiles. "Now," she went on, "tell me about this. You say you're going to have the other Welcome girl here. How do you expect to arrange that?"

Druce grinned triumphantly. "That's dead easy," he said. "You see I'm married to her." He had expected to startle Miss Masters with this information, but he was disappointed. She merely arched her brows slightly. "Then you marry them, do you?" "Yes, when I have to. It's the easiest way." "Then this girl—Elsie—is living in your—a—a—hotel?"

"No," replied Druce hesitatingly, "she's gone away." Then he added quickly, "but she'll be back."

"Gone away? I don't understand." "Oh, we had a family row this morning. I told her that if she wanted to get along in Chicago she'd have to discard her Millville morals and be a good fellow. She's squeamish. I let her understand that she'd have to—"

"I see," said Miss Masters. "She thought that, because she was your wife she wouldn't have to drink with the patrons in your cafe. When you told her she'd have to, she got angry and walked out. Is that it?"

"You're wise," replied Druce admiringly.

"You say she'll be back. How do you know that?"

"I know it, because she hasn't got a dime. With her it's a case of coming back or starving to death in the Levee, and I know enough about her to be sure she'll be back. She can't get away from me."

"And the other girl, Patience?"

"She thinks this is a sort of a music hall. She's coming here with her mother Saturday night. Before she discovers that this place isn't exactly what she believes it is, Harry Boland will see her up there on the stand with the rest of my talent. I'll get the girl out of the place before he can talk to her. That will put the kibosh on their love affair."

"What do you expect to do with these girls afterward?"

"Oh, we have facilities here"—Druce's smile was evil—"for breaking 'em in. Afterward—well, I don't know. It may be dangerous to keep them around Chicago. I can get a good price for them." He laughed. "You know I'm a dealer in live stock."

"Yes, yes, you expect to sell them. That's not a bad idea."

"Now look here, kid," said Druce, "you've asked me a lot of questions and got fair answers. It's a poor game that can't be played both ways. I want to know something about you."

Miss Masters curled herself up comfortably in a corner of the booth. She looked challengingly at Druce.

"Shoot," she said.

"Now, who are you?"

"You know my name. It's Masters."

"I don't mean that. What are you?"

Miss Masters replied quickly, "I—why—I'm a girl, and—you say yourself I'm wise."

"You don't have to tell me that. Where did you come from? Where did Boland get you?"

"Before I went to work for Boland I was in St. Louis."

"What did you do there?"

"Oh, I shan't answer that question—yet."

"Well, you seem to know a great deal about the kind of business I'm in. Where did you get your information?"

"Picked it up."

"In St. Louis?"

"Yes, I learned some things there."

"Have you ever been in this business?"

"What business?"

"Well, this cafe business—and the rest of it."

"You say I know a good deal about it."

"Yes, you know a lot about it. And you've got your information from the inside. And Boland knows you know a lot about it. Otherwise he wouldn't have sent you down here."

"Yes?" Miss Masters was silent for a moment. "Druce," she went on, "did you ever hear of the Broughton Club?"

"Sure, that swell joint in St. Louis?"

"Yes. Well, I'm interested in it."

"As owner?"

"Never mind about that. I'm interested in it and one of my reasons for calling on you is to get some girls for the club."

"You want to buy some girls?"

"You said it."

"From me?"

"From you, if I can get the right figures. If I can't, I'll try elsewhere. You're not the only 'dealer in live stock' in the Levee."

"I'll make the figures right."

"I'm interested in this place."

"In the Cafe Sinister?"

"Yes, I want to know something about your methods. We don't know it all in St. Louis. I think I can pick up a little information here. I'm going back to St. Louis in a month. I want to take some girls back with me, and I'd like to find out just how a first class joint like the Cafe Sinister is operated in Chicago."

"Is this a proposition?"

"Yes, it's a proposition."

"All right. Go on."

"I want to live at the Cafe Sinister during the week our deal for the lease is on. I'll take rooms in your—a—hotel, upstairs.

"And I'll be around the cafe, and making myself at home generally," added Miss Masters, reassuringly.

"Go as far as you like," answered Druce, "and if you need a body guard," he added, with a knowing wink, "why, you know me."

Miss Masters' eyes narrowed. "I told you I could look out for myself," she answered.

"You'll have to look out for yourself," retorted Druce significantly.

"Let me do the worrying about that."

Druce was silent. He had determined to accept Miss Masters' offer. He felt that she was walking into his trap and yet, so great had grown his respect for her that he did not know his next move.

"I'll have a suite prepared for you," he said.

"That's settled, then."

Miss Masters got up from her seat. As she did so Druce attempted a caress. "I'm going to collect part of the rent in advance," he said.

"Are you?" Miss Masters pushed him away sharply. He did not repeat his indiscretion. Instead he stood back respectfully to let her pass. In the palm of her hand with the muzzle pointing firmly in his direction he saw a small, steel-blue magazine pistol. The girl's finger was on the trigger.

"If you'll have one of your servants show me the suite," said Miss Masters, "I'll telephone for my maid."

Then she added, seemingly as an afterthought,

"I never pay the rent, Mr. Druce, until the end of the week."

CHAPTER XX

DRUCE SIGNS A SIGNIFICANT DOCUMENT

Mary Randall realized that she was playing a dangerous game. She had placed herself in Druce's power because taking that risk had seemed to her the best way to gather evidence against the Cafe Sinister. She had not acted without laying her plans carefully. Her whole campaign for the week that she was to be in Druce's dive had been mapped out before she set foot so unexpectedly inside his door.

The girl depended upon two things for protection. First was Druce's fear of the power of John Boland. She believed that the man would not dare to use physical violence against her if he thought she was what she had represented herself to be—John Boland's agent. Second was his desire for a renewal of the lease to the cafe. Mary was confident that Druce would plot against her but she was equally sure he would not move until after the lease had been signed. If both these protections failed, she still had her magazine pistol. And she knew how to use it.

In coming into Druce's place she had deliberately counted on the ascendancy which she knew her beauty and her air of mystery had obtained over him. She was playing the pander at his own game. It was an extremely dangerous game but she believed she could beat him. And the results would be worth the risk.

Meanwhile her greatest anxiety was to prevent Druce from communicating in any way with John Boland. If Druce should learn through Boland that he had not delegated her to negotiate the lease, that she was in fact Mary Randall, then she would be face to face with a fight for her life. But she was quite sure that Druce would not communicate with Boland. She knew the workings of Boland's office well enough to understand how difficult it was for Druce to get a word with the master of the Electric Trust and as a special precaution she had put an inhibition upon him not to call at or telephone to the office. Finally, before she had quite finished with Boland, she had arranged with his telephone operator that no calls from Druce should be put on John Boland's wire.

Mary's first move after she had been shown to her suite was to telephone to Anna, her maid, whom she had left nearby before making her visit to the cafe. Anna arrived in a short time with a porter carrying a couple of heavy suit cases.

When the two girls were at last alone in their rooms they began preparing for their week's stay by making a thorough examination of the locks on the doors. They found them secure. Then, closing the keyholes, they proceeded to unpack the suit cases. Out of them they took, besides various articles of apparel, a complete dictagraph apparatus. The transmitter was hidden under a mat on a table in the reception room that formed part of the suite. The wires were carried down the leg of the table and under the carpets to a small closet; there Anna installed a small table, a pocket electric light and her stenographer's notebook. A small camera was hidden in one of the window curtains. It was focused so as to take in the space surrounding the table in the reception room. When one of the curtains was raised the plate was automatically exposed and the raising of the curtain at the same time let enough light into the room to take an excellent picture.

With these arrangements completed, Mary began a tour of the cafe building. She found Druce eager to serve her. By him she was guided to every part of the place, meeting the people she wanted to know and learning all of the details of the infamous business in which Druce, Anson and Boland were jointly embarked. For three days she went about these tours of inspection undisturbed. In the evenings she had the women habitues of the place in her rooms, talking to them as if she were one of their own kind and learning from them the squalid stories of their downfall and the part Druce and Anson had played in it. Anna was not in sight during any of these interviews. She was seated at the little table with the dictagraph at her ear, her fountain pen in her hand and her stenographer's notebook before her. Nothing that was said escaped her.

Meanwhile Druce was having an unpleasant time with Anson. He had tried at first to keep from him the fact of Miss Masters' residence in their "hotel." "The mastiff," however, was not long deceived. When he confronted Druce with what he had learned, Druce with an assumption of frankness told him of his interview with Miss Masters and attempted to reassure him.

Anson, however, was by nature suspicious. "I don't like it," he snarled. "You've let a spy into the house."

Druce tried at first to argue with him. Then he grew angry. Finally he turned on his partner.

"You mind your own business," he advised him, white with rage. "I'll manage this thing. The girl's mine. I'm going to have her. Keep away from her. By God, if you interfere with my schemes I'll kill you."

Anson was not terrified by this threat. He knew that in any physical encounter he was more than a match for the slender Druce. But he feared to quarrel with his partner. He was too appreciative of Druce's value to him and their enterprise to want to lose him. He growled a smothered string of curses, but Druce had his way.

Druce had become so much infatuated with Miss Masters that he had thrown caution to the winds. Never before in his life had he been under the influence of any woman. Now that such an influence had seized him he was overwhelmed by it. He had arrived perilously close to the point where, if he had known the true character of the woman he was sheltering, his infatuation would have led him to risk the danger merely to have her near him. His thoughts were on her constantly, his mind busy during every waking hour on schemes for, entrapping her.

Mary had taken up her abode in the Cafe Sinister on Monday. On Thursday she sent for Druce. He came to her suite eagerly.

He found Miss Masters sitting at the table in the reception room. He sat down opposite her and facing the window at her invitation.

"Druce," said the girl, "I've sent for you because I want to close that deal for the girls I spoke to you about."

"The girls you're going to take back to St. Louis?"

"Yes, I'll want five or six."

"You've been looking over my stock?" said Druce with a leer.

"Yes," replied Miss Masters, concealing her repulsion.

"Well, I guess we can come to terms. Who do you want?"

"I only care for four of the girls I have seen," replied Miss Masters. "I want that little girl, Maida, the blonde girl you call Luella, Clara, and that young brunette, Esther."

"Gee," said Druce, "you don't want much, do you? Why those are the youngest and prettiest girls we've got in the place. That Luella has only been in the district three weeks. All the rest of them are new ones."

"I know it. That's why I want them."

"They'll cost you money."

"I expect to pay money for them."

"I want $200 apiece for those four girls." The price was high. Druce thought Miss Masters would reject it.

"Very well," returned Miss Masters. "That will be $800."

"You're willing to pay it?"

"Yes. I'm going to spend $1,000 with you."

"Four ain't enough?"

"No, I'm going to take two more, if I can get them. You say you expect to have these Welcome sisters?"

"Sure, I'll have them."

"Well, you told me you didn't want to run the risk of keeping them around Chicago. I'll take them off your hands."

"You expect to get them for $200?"

"Certainly. You don't know yet that you can deliver. Has the one you married come back?"

"Oh, I'll deliver."

"I'm not as sure of that as you are, but I'm willing to speculate on it. I'll make you this proposition. I'll write you a check for $1,000 and take my chance on you delivering the six girls I name."

"No checks go," said Druce.

"You'll have to take a check if you do business with me."

Druce considered. He wanted the $1,000. He did not want to quarrel with Miss Masters. He capitulated.

"Write the check," he said.

Miss Masters took a check-book from a drawer and drew a check, payable to Druce. She handed it to him. He looked at the paper doubtfully.

"I'll have to indorse that," he said.

Miss Masters laughed.

"Certainly," she said, "you'll have to indorse it unless you want to keep it as a souvenir." She smiled at him. "Druce," she said, "you'll never get along in this business if you're a coward."

"It's direct evidence against me."

"You don't trust me?"

"All right, girlie. I'll trust you." He folded the check and put it in his pocket.

"Now, we'll have to have a bit of writing."

"No writing for mine," retorted Druce. "This check is plenty."

"Oh, Mr. Druce," Miss Masters spoke appealingly. "You don't think that's fair, do you? You've got my check."

"I guess it's you that's not trusting me now," said Druce.

"But you admit yourself that you may not deliver."

"No I don't. I will deliver."

"But this isn't business."

"It's the way we do this kind of business in Chi."

Miss Masters got up from the table, as if exasperated.

"Look here, Mr. Druce," she said. "How can signing an agreement covering this sale hurt you? Oh, what a lot of cowards you 'live stock dealers' are! Can't you see that if you sign this agreement with me I'm incriminated as well as you are? The Mann act gets the buyer as well as the seller."

"Well, what's the agreement?"

"It says simply this: 'In consideration of $1,000 I agree to deliver two days from date the following girls'—I'll write in their names—'to Miss Masters.'"

"You're not trying to put anything over?"

"Did it ever strike you that by selling these girls to me you'd have John Boland where you wanted him?"

"Boland?"

"I'm his agent."

"All right." Druce snatched up the paper and read it. "Write in the names." Miss Masters wrote the names of six girls into the document. She handed it back to Druce and picked up a pen.

"Just a moment," she said, giving him the pen. "It's dark here. I'll raise the curtain."

She stepped quickly across the room and adjusted the curtain so that the sunlight fell full across Druce as he signed his name to the agreement. As he finished the last stroke he heard a faint "click."

"What was that?" he demanded anxiously.

"The curtain caught on the window latch," replied Miss Masters. She picked up the agreement and blotted the signature. "Thank you," she said, "now I've got something for my $1,000."

Druce laughed uneasily. The maid, Anna, entered from an

adjoining apartment. Druce realized uncomfortably that the interview was over.

"Well," he said, going to the door and smiling sentimentally at Miss Masters, "so long. See you later."

"Yes," replied Miss Masters in a tone he didn't just like, "I'll see you later."

CHAPTER XXI

DRUCE PROVES A TRUE PROPHET

Saturday night begins at the Cafe Sinister at nine o'clock. At that hour the twin columns of glass at its portal are lighted and the Levee pours the first of its revelers into the spacious ground floor drinking room. The orchestra strikes up the first of its syncopated melodies; the barkeepers arrange their polished glasses in glittering rows; the waiters, soft-footed and watchful, take their places at their appointed stations.

The revelers come in an order regulated by inexorable circumstance. In the van are the women with the professional escorts, haggard creatures who have served their time in the district and who are on the brink of that oblivion which means starvation and slow death. Youth and health have flown and now no paint nor cosmetic can cloak their real character. They must come early because their need of money is bitter and a watchful eye for opportunity must take the place of the physical allurement that once made life in the tenderloin so easy. They sink into their seats and wait, contemptuous of their escorts, and yet pitifully dependent upon them. For without the escorts they cannot enter the Cafe Sinister. That is a tribute which the rulers of the tenderloin, through them, pays tribute to the majesty of the law.

A group of hardened rounders follows. These are men to whom the Cafe Sinister and the district have become a habit. They bring with them women of their own kind—women who, through years of dissipation, have still, like misers, managed to hoard some trace of bloom. They drink deeply, for the men are spenders. The wine flows free and the talk grows loud. Occasionally a man quarrels profanely with his companion and a soft-footed waiter with a thug's face whispers him to sullen silence.

An hour flies by. Now the Levee, roused from its sodden, day-long slumber, is wide awake. The way between the twin pillars at the Cafe Sinister's entrance is choked with the flood of merry-makers. These newcomers are not so easy to classify as their predecessors. They are the crowd from the street,—the thief with his girl pal, eager to spend the plunder of their last successful exploit; the big corporation's entertainer, out to show a party of country customers the sights of a great city; the visitor from afar, lonely and seeking excitement; the man about town, the respectable woman who with a trusted male confidant seeks shady and clandestine amusement; college students with unspoiled appetites off for a lark; women of the district still new enough to the life of vice to find pleasure in its excitements; periodical drinkers out for a night of it; clerks, cashiers, bookkeepers, schoolboys and roues.

And here and there, weaving in and out through this heterogeneous mob lurks the pander seeking for his prey— the ignorant young girl, trembling on the verge of her first step into the depths, the little lost sister of tomorrow.

By ten o'clock the merry making in the Cafe Sinister had attained the vociferousness of a riot. As the swift-footed waiters passed more and more liquor about, the voices of the speakers rose higher and higher. At last the orchestra itself could scarcely be heard. The singers, half maudlin themselves, and knowing they could not be heard above the universal din, abandoned harmony and resorted to shouts and suggestive gyrations. A woman fell helplessly into the arms of her escort who, gloating, winked knowingly at a male companion. Another drunkenly attempted to dance and was restrained by the waiters. An elderly reprobate, convoying two unsteady young girls, importuned Druce for one of his private dining rooms.

Druce and Anson watched over the revelers and directed the entertainers. "The Mastiff," comfortably full of his favorite liquor, whisky, glowered on the crowd with as near an aspect of good nature as he was able to muster. Druce, who knew his own success in business was due to alertness of mind and who was almost an ascetic in the matter of drink, was no less at peace with the world.

"Money in that crowd," rumbled the huge Anson.

"Yes," replied Druce, "business is mighty good."

"How about our lease?"

"The blow-off comes tonight."

"You're sure of your plans?"

"I am, if young Boland shows up."

"Well, he'll be here?"

"Yes, I wrote him an anonymous letter telling him if he wanted to see his girl, he could find her singing at the Cafe Sinister."

"That ought to fetch him. How about the old man?"

"He sent me word today that he'd be here and that he'd dropped hints to the son he'd heard some bad stuff about the girl."

"You haven't talked to him?"

"No; I got my orders. I stayed away."

"How about the Welcome kid you married?"

"She's down and out. I sent one of our cappers early in the week to look her up. Somebody'd slipped her a lone five dollar bill. She woke up yesterday morning broke. I don't know where she's eating, but I've sent word through the district to keep her hungry. She'll be in tonight."

Druce spoke with indifference, but the truth was that he was not at all sure that Elsie Welcome would return. He had begun to respect the girl's strength of character. He had scarcely finished his sentence when he gave a gasp of relief.

"Ah-h!" he muttered.

"What's that?" demanded Anson.

"Here she comes now."

As they looked down through the drinking room they saw the slender figure of a girl approaching. She came slowly, supporting her wavering steps with the backs of the revelers' chairs. Her face was pale and desperately haggard. Several of the men as she passed clutched at her skirts and shouted invitations at her. She tore herself away from them and made straight for the place where Druce and Anson were standing.

For a moment, Druce almost felt sorry for her.

"You're back, kid?" he said softly.

"Yes," replied the girl, fiercely.

"You're going to be good?"

Elsie burst out sobbing. It was her last struggle.

"Come now, Elsie," Druce spoke almost tenderly. "Don't snivel."

"Martin," the girl gasped appealingly. "O, my God! Be kind to me."

"Don't worry about me, girlie. You forget that Sunday school stuff and you'll get along with me fine. You're hungry, aren't you, kid?"

"I'm starving," replied the girl.

"Come with me. I'll have the chef get you a big feed. After that I want you to come back and do what I tell you. I won't be hard on you, kid. You'll not have to work tonight. All I'll want you to do is sit up on the stand with my other entertainers."

Elsie was too broken in spirit to reply. She followed her master dumbly. He led her to one of his small private dining rooms, arranged a seat for her and turned on the lights. Then he went back to the kitchen to order the girl's meal.

After Druce had left, Elsie folded her arms on the table and cushioning her head on them, began to weep softly. Druce returned with the food, kissed her to take the sting from the feed, which both he and she knew was the price of her shame, and left her. The girl ate ravenously. Afterward she fell into an uneasy slumber against the cushions of the booth.

She was awakened by someone entering the room. Looking up, she saw the bowed figure and gray hair of an elderly woman. The intruder carried a bucket of hot water in one hand and a mop in the other. She had come into the booth thinking it unoccupied, and did not see Elsie until she was very close to her.

"I beg your pardon," she said, dropping her mop and bucket and starting back.

Elsie stared at her. Then she stood up, her face pale as death, her eyes starting like the eyes of one who has seen a vision.

"Mother!" she screamed. "Oh, God! Mother!" and flung herself into her mother's arms.

CHAPTER XXII

"THE MILLS OF THE GODS"

After Druce left Elsie he went back to his favorite station behind the musicians' stand. He had been there only a moment when he saw the elder Boland enter. Boland came in quietly through a side door and stood looking about inquiringly.

Druce silently summoned a waiter and sent him to Boland with a message. A little later the two men were in Druce's private office alone and the door was closed. They sat down at a table.

"Well," said Druce, "I see you're on time."

"Yes," replied Boland coldly. "I make it a point to keep my engagements. Your arrangements are complete, I suppose. I haven't heard a word from you all week."

There was a petulance in his tone the reason for which Druce did not comprehend.

"It's going to work out all right. One of the Welcome girls is here now. I'm expecting the other." He pushed an electric button. A waiter appeared.

"Go out and ask the professor if that new entertainer I'm expecting has arrived," he ordered.

The waiter was gone but a few seconds.

"She's come," he reported. "She's up on the stand and will go on right after the intermission."

"That's her," said Druce to Boland. The waiter vanished.

"Good," said Boland. "Druce," he went on, "I'm pleased with the way you've handled this. Here's something to prove it." He took a document from his breast pocket and passed it across the table. It was the lease.

"Thanks," said Druce, keenly pleased by an inspection of the papers, "that looks good to me."

"It's yours," returned Boland, "but of course I expect you to carry out your part of the contract."

"How about Harry?"

"No need to worry about that. He'll be here."

"Well, we're waiting on him."

There was a pause. Neither man seemed to know how to continue the conversation. Druce broke the silence.

"Boland," he asked, "what have you got against this girl?"

Boland resented the question, but was compelled to answer.

"She wants to marry my son. I don't think she's fit to marry him. If she were, she wouldn't be in a place like this."

Druce laughed unpleasantly.

"You know very well," he replied, "that she wouldn't be here if I hadn't managed it for you."

Boland made no reply for this. Druce went on.

"Tell me," he demanded, "on the square, now, is that all you've got against this girl?"

"Just what do you mean by that, Druce?" demanded Boland, eying him calmly.

"Didn't you know the Welcomes before this girl came into your son's life?"

Boland turned very pale.

"That's an idiotic question," he answered. "How would a man in my position know people like the Welcomes?"

"When I was in Millville," replied Druce evenly, "I heard a good deal about old Tom Welcome. It seems that someone stole an invention from him."

"Just why should I be interested in that story?"

"I don't know," replied Druce. "It just struck me that you might be. There was no harm in asking, was there?"

Boland ignored the question.

"Look here," he said, changing the subject, "suppose you get this lease from me, are you sure you can continue doing business as you are without police interference?"

Druce laughed and picked up the receiver of the telephone which stood on the table. There was an attachment that enabled Boland to hear at the same time. He handed the second receiver to the master of the Electric Trust.

"What's the idea?" inquired Boland.

"I'm just going to answer your question."

He called for a number.

"That's police station R," said Boland.

"I know," replied Druce, "just listen."

"Hello," he said presently, "is this you, Cap?"

Boland heard a familiar voice answer affirmatively.

"This is Druce talking," the dive-owner went on, "Druce of the Cafe Sinister. Say, we'll be open all night tonight. Don't make any trouble for us, you understand. Just let your fellows know that they're not to hear anything that goes on in this beat. I'll send McEdwards around in the morning with a special envelope for you. Get me?"

Druce cut off the two telephones.

"Well," he asked triumphantly, "what do you think of that?"

Boland laughed cynically.

"Rather good," he answered. "I know your friend, the captain. The fact is, I know him rather well. We belong to the same church." He chuckled over his own joke. "However," he went on, "I didn't come here to be entertained, nor to be initiated into the mysteries of the police department. Let's get down to business. I've got to get out of town tonight. I'm going to 'Frisco."

"To 'Frisco?"

"Yes, I'm in a mess. Mary Randall—"

"Randall! Boland, don't tell me you're scared of that woman, too."

"Man alive, haven't you heard? She got into my office in disguise and stole a lot of my papers. I don't know just yet what she's got, but I've decided to hunt seclusion for a while."

"She was disguised?"

"Yes, she came into my office as private secretary. I trusted her implicitly. You'll remember her. She gave the name of Miss Masters."

Druce stood up with an exclamation. His face had gone white and he clutched at the table for support. Boland stared at him in astonishment.

"What's hit you?" he demanded.

Druce made no reply. Through his mind was passing the panorama of how he had delivered himself bound hand and foot to the girl he thought he was entrapping. Suddenly, he turned and dashed in a frenzy out of the room. He was bound, with murder in his heart, for Miss Masters' suite.

As he came tearing out of the office he found himself suddenly seized and halted.

"Let me go," screamed Druce, "damn you, let me go."

He fought to release himself, but vainly. He looked up into the face of Harry Boland.

"What's your hurry?" inquired young Boland coolly. "Don't be in a rush. I want to ask you a few questions."

He produced a letter from his pocket. Druce recognized it at a glance as the anonymous note he had written to lure young Boland to the cafe.

"Did you write that?" demanded Boland.

Druce struggled in a frenzy.

"To hell with you and your questions," he yelled. "Let me by or I'll kill you."

He grappled with Boland and the two men wrestled out to the edge of the big drinking room.

"You wrote it," Boland hissed in his ear.

"It's a lie. I'm going to give you the beating of your life."

The elder Boland, who had followed Druce, fell upon his son. Harry turned and recognized his father.

"You here?" he demanded, facing his parent.

"Yes," replied John Boland, "I'm here. I came, because I had been informed that you were to meet a woman of the tenderloin in this place; and when I find you, I find you fighting with a dive-keeper."

Harry dropped the struggling Druce and turned on his father.

"What do you mean?" he asked, defiantly.

"I mean just that," replied John Boland. He turned toward the musicians' stand and pointed dramatically at Patience Welcome, who, her face almost as pale as her white lace gown, was advancing toward the front of the platform to sing.

Harry Boland's face went white as hers.

The words he gasped were drowned by a cry, Elsie Welcome, coming for the first time since her return to Druce into the drinking room, saw her sister standing upon the rostrum, poised to sing.

"Patience! Patience!" she screamed in a voice of despair. "Oh, my sister, what brought you to this place?"

She fell to the floor fainting. The whole cafe was in an uproar.

Carter Anson, roused to fury by the disturbance, fought his way through the crowd to the place where he had seen her fall.

Druce, escaped from Harry Boland, struggled from another angle to make his way through the mob. As if by magic half a score of policemen suddenly hemmed in the fighting mass. Druce, struggling blindly to make a pathway for himself, suddenly looked up to see Mary Randall standing on a table on the opposite side of the room directing the police. A wave of maniacal anger overwhelmed him. In a flash his hand went to his pocket and reappeared with a pistol.

There was an explosion, a man's yell of rage, followed by a choking gulp of mortal anguish. Druce was seized and flung to the floor.

At the same moment Mary Randall, leaping down from her table, ran to the center of the room. Carter Anson lay there, struggling through his last throes,—the bullet in his brain.

CHAPTER XXIII

AFTER THE TRAGEDY

Mary Randall stood beside the dead body of Carter Anson. Such tragedy had not entered into her plans, nor had she conceived what it might be to see a man die bearing the bullet intended for her own intrepid heart. A strange numbness possessed her faculties.

She heard the voice of Mrs. Welcome beside her. The mother was speaking with anguished entreaty to Elsie. The girl had risen to her feet and was gazing with a dreadful fascination at Druce, writhing in the grasp of the officers who seized him.

"Come, Miss Randall," one of her police aids said to the reformer. "This is no place for you—now."

"There must be something I can do," she spoke with a flash of her usual energy, then laid her hand on Mrs. Welcome's arm.

"Harvey Spencer is here," she said. "There he is trying to get through the crowd to us now. Perhaps he can help you to persuade your daughter to go away with you."

Elsie Welcome looked at Mary Randall, who was destined never to forget the pitiful revelation of the girl's dark eyes. Mary Randall read that despair of the lost mingled with woman's intense clinging to the man she has chosen,—her strange stubborn clinging, when, entangled, she hears an echo of happier and purer love.

"How dare you meddle in people's affairs like this and put us into such dreadful trouble?" Elsie asked of the one who would help her. Then to her mother, pulling away from her longing clasp, "You understand that at a time like this my place is with my husband."

Elsie doubled under the arms which would have detained her and ran out of the cafe.

"Go to Millville, Mrs. Welcome, back to your old home, as soon you can. Let me look after Elsie. Go to this boarding-house (handing her a card). Go there with Patience tonight, and I will send you some money tomorrow." Miss Randall spoke quickly, and before Mrs. Welcome realized it, had hurried in pursuit of Elsie.

But Elsie Welcome had disappeared.

Mary Randall found herself standing, as all who work for those who sin and suffer must often stand, baffled by evil's resistance. Saddened by somewhat of a divine sadness, Mary went across to the rendezvous where her faithful Anna awaited her and left the field.

Harvey Spencer came to her downtown office early next day. He found her surrounded by her strongest allies, already in conference as to the best means of pursuing their crusade which had aroused Chicago with the startling news of The Raid of Mary Randall on the Cafe Sinister, headlined in the morning newspapers.

Harvey Spencer had taken Mrs. Welcome to the boarding-house designated by Miss Randall where she was joined by Patience—and of Patience you shall know presently. The remainder of the night, or most of it, he spent trying to learn what had become of Elsie.

"I thought she might be still in that—hotel, as they call it," Harvey, haggard with his night's search, told Miss Randall. "I went to the jail too, but of course they would not let her inside there so late, even if she had wanted to."

"She is sure to go there today to see Druce. Try again, Mr. Spencer, when you go out from here," said Miss Randall.

"And keep you eye on Druce. Nobody will suspect you of being a detective. You can telephone here if you see any activity around him," said a clever special from headquarters.

"Good scheme," commended the journalist, another of Mary Randall's strongest aids.

Harvey Spencer made notes of the right steps to take and, thanking Miss Randall with a curious humility, went out again on his quest.

"Now we must learn what the vice-moneymakers will try to do next," said a former high official in the municipality. "Our one safe bet is that they will all get together and that John Boland, the boss of the bunch, will map out the fight against us."

"Is it a losing fight?" asked a famous banker, known among his intimates as the hard-headed enthusiast.

Virginia Brooks

"Right against wrong can never be permanently a losing fight," quietly said a small muscular clergyman from the northwest side.

"It has taken two thousand years for mankind to begin this fight against buying and selling young virgins who can be coaxed or thrust into the market-place," said Mary Randall. "We must fight on, even in one seemingly losing field. It is not to be believed that the people of this nation will be content to submit very much longer to the presence of a band of prowling wolves tolerated by courts and protected by rascally lawyers whose acknowledged trade is to destroy virtue,—the latent motherhood of young women,—whose whole activity is directed to the exploitation of our little lost sisters."

"Chicago has to lead the fight, as she has been one of the leaders in the trade," said the banker. "Now, for our next step!"

CHAPTER XXIV

"THE HIGHWAY OF THE UPRIGHT"

Up to the moment when he heard the report of Druce's pistol and saw Carter Anson fall, Harry Boland's whole being had been concentrated in a consuming horror at sight of Patience Welcome in the Cafe Sinister.

The crack of the pistol restored his composure. He saw clearly the infamy of the plot against her,—and against himself. One of the conspirators was already dead on the scene of this last of many crimes. Druce was struggling with the police, taking him for murder of Anson, his partner.

John Boland, the third conspirator, faced his son in a desperate composure.

"Come, Harry, we must get out of here. It will never do to be seen here—"

"For you!" Harry shook off his father's hand upon his arm. "Go, by all means! I shall take care of myself." He walked towards the singers' platform beyond the seething crowd.

John Boland believed of himself afterwards that he would have followed Harry, but at the moment he saw a bowed and gray-haired woman before him, great fear and horror on her face, pressing her way in from scrubbing in the booths beyond. The mop and bucket with which she had been working were in either hand. At sight of his face she dropped her tools of toil and clutched his coat. It was Tom Welcome's widow.

He uttered a cry like a beast of prey as he shook her off; but he felt himself shiver, conscience making him a coward, and he hurried out, reaching by an exit the alley leading to a side street.

A police lieutenant suddenly barred his way.

"Not so fast there," said the functionary.

Boland recognized the man as an officer whom he had once placed under obligation to him.

"Good evening, Murphy."

"Mr. Boland!"

"Yes. I was passing and heard the shot. You understand, of course, that I wish to avoid being seen here. Do you know where I can find a taxi?"

The policeman turned and summoned a taxicab with a gesture. Boland got in at the open door. He leaned forward and spoke with peculiar force, although very low:

"If my son, Harry Boland, happens to pass by here, see that he gets into a taxi whose driver will bring him to my house, to my house, remember, no matter what address he gives."

"I understand, sir." Probably the young man's been misbehaving, was what he thought.

"Pay the driver—in advance—with this, or part of it," continued Mr. Boland.

"Thank you, sir; thank you. I understand."

Boland's car scuttled away into the darkness.

Harry Boland, pushing through the crowd to Patience, saw the futile effort of Mrs. Welcome to take Elsie from the place. He heard Mary Randall's brief direction and spoke reassuringly to the anguished mother as he pressed a friendly hand on her slight shoulder.

"I will see that Spencer takes you to that boarding-house, where you will be comfortable until you can get away. I will bring Patience. We may get there before you arrive."

As John Boland foresaw, it was but a few moments after his own departure before Harry Boland reached the street looking for a conveyance. He was assisting Patience Welcome. Rather, she was clinging to him, sobbing like a frightened child. The shooting that had interrupted her pathetic attempt to sing was only part of the tragedy to her.

"I—I saw my little sister in there," she sobbed. "She called me by name. And such a pathetic cry. Did you hear it?" Patience was sadly unnerved and ill.

"Hush, dear one," Harry soothed her. "Your mother, Harvey and Miss Randall are there, you know. Whatever can be done, they will do. You are my one and only care, and just now, dearest girl, you're ill. I'll take you to the place where your mother is going. Now, please stop crying; try—try—

everything will be all right."

A taxicab appeared, the chauffeur seemingly having anticipated that he was wanted. Harry got in, half carrying
Patience, and expecting to be stopped by an officer. But no
policeman seemed to see or hear him as he gave the driver
the address of the old-fashioned boarding-house selected by
Mary Randall.

They rode in silence. Patience sat apart from him, breathing
deeply of the fresh air at the window of the car as they
rushed swiftly through the city streets. Slowly he felt the
tension of the situation released. It was as if the dazed girl
were freed from the physical mesh which had been thrown
about her.

Then she spoke quite calmly, in her natural voice, but very
slowly:

"Harry, I once dreamed that I was in terrible trouble and that
you came and helped me. Are you sure I am not dreaming
now?"

"Is it a happy dream, if you are, my darling?"

"I—I don't know," faltered Patience. "It is wonderful to be
here with—you."

"Do you trust me, Patience? Do you trust me when I tell you
that I care more for you than I ever knew I could care for
anybody?"

"Yes," she whispered.

"I want to make you happy. I want to love you and work for
you and have you for my wife, and make a home with you."

"Harry!" She slipped her hand into his.

"Harry, I still feel afraid. It was such a dreadful thing to see. Was that man killed? It was he who asked me to sing. They had been disappointed about getting a singer, he said, and he gave me ten dollars. All that money for a few songs—it seemed like stealing. But I took it. Mother helped put on this dress they gave me to sing in. You know I went there to help mother clean the place. And to think we saw a murder!"

"My poor darling!" Something in his voice caused her to put her hand up to his face. He felt her finger tips on his eyelids, then down his wet cheeks.

"My poor darling!" She put her arm around his neck—then their trembling lips met.

Harry was the first to speak. "All that you have gone through brings us closer together than anything else in life possibly could, Patience. I am so proud of you and so down on myself that I ever let you out of my sight—"

"You must not be down on my—"

"Say it, dear! I want to hear my sweetheart say the word."

"I was going to say 'my dearest,' but I'll say,—if you want me to,—my—my husband."

"You dear, sweet wife!" responded Harry.

After a few moments Harry observed that they were being taken farther than he had directed the man to go. The boarding-house was rather close to town. He found that they were well on the north side, nearing the quarter of his father's house. He called to stop the driver, but the man remained deaf to his efforts, except to increase the speed, and presently drew up at the Boland mansion.

"How dare you bring me here?" Harry demanded, stepping out of the car to remonstrate.

"Orders."

"Orders! I ordered you where I wanted you to go. Here, if you need two fares for one job, you swindler! Hold on—"

"Driver! Come here."

Harry heard his father's stern voice from the opened doorway. "Driver! Take that girl wherever she wants to go. Harry, come in here! It's time for a show-down."

"It certainly is time for a show-down!" Harry assisted Patience from the car. "You may wait and earn the fare I just paid you or go to jail," he said to the driver, and boldly led Patience into his father's house.

The elder Boland turned into a den at the right of the front hallway and closed the door. He looked at Patience with an appraising glance, then kindly at his son.

"I suppose you must be humored in this affair," he said in an indulgent manner, "while you haven't sense to see that the present is scarcely the time to devote yourself to any such young woman. What do you say to a trip to California? I'll foot all the bills, and later I will settle what you ask for on you." He spoke to Patience.

"Thank you." She spoke without a tremor. "You may do something substantial for my mother, because you—took— my poor father's invention. Do you know, sir, that my poor father never recovered from that loss?"

"Hell's fire!" yelled John Boland, "I—"

"You see, sir," interrupted Harry deliberately, "it really is time for a show-down. I wouldn't go away from Chicago at present, even for the wedding journey which we will pretend you were honestly offering us. I am going to stay and fight it out. You will have to stay and fight it out, too."

"Me?" blustered Boland. "What have I got to fight out?"

"You know very well why you were at Druce's cafe tonight. You were in a plot against me, leagued with that fellow, Druce, and his tribe, too, against the crusade started by Mary Randall to protect girls. You prefer to make money exploiting them. Not directly, perhaps, but conspicuously indirect."

"So you are turning traitor in—politics?" sneered his father. "Taking sides with a crazy fanatic, whose presence at the cafe caused the death of a good citizen of Chicago. Druce did not mean to shoot Anson."

"I see your line of defense. It's you who have turned traitor—to all that is right in you as a man. See, here is the anonymous letter which summoned me to the cafe tonight. I wish you could tell me that you do not know who wrote that note."

Boland read the letter scornfully. "How should I know who writes you letters? Young men who make alliances with women who frequent such places must expect such messages," he sneered.

"Stop!" Harry's eyes blazed with anger. "We have borne all that we shall of that sort from you. One more such syllable and I shall not be able to speak to you as to my father—even in outward respect."

"You seem already to have forgotten that completely."

Harry let the sneer pass. "It is up to you, sir, to decide now—this moment—whether or not I ever look upon you as my father again. I have myself decided that I shall no longer be a party to your crimes."

"Crimes! My God, this is too much!"

"You are too shrewd a man to have a fool for a son. I see plainly that you were leagued with Druce and Anson to blacken the woman I love. But right is might and love is right. The whole dastardly affair enlightens me as to the nature of your alliance with that dive. Why did you renew the lease to Druce against my protest? I never realized until tonight the horror of your extensive holdings of tenderloin property. I don't want another cent from such sources."

"Very well." The elder Boland shook with anger. "Get out of this house, you and your—fitting mate. Never let me see your face again. Tomorrow I will undertake a campaign which will brand you among your friends as a son who turned traitor to his father in his hour of stress. All my power, all my money, will be against you. I will crush you as I have every man who has dared oppose me. Get out of my house!"

Harry gazed at his father in a tumult of pity and wrath, but he did not speak.

Patience, her eyes filled with tears, her hands nervously clutching her 'kerchief, walked up to the angry man.

"I am sorry for you," she said, "just as I always used to be sorry for my poor father when he was drunk as you are now with your own anger. You know that I *am* a fitting mate for your son. I don't understand your enmity unless it's because we're not rich like you."

Harry caught Patience in his arms. "Remember, it makes no difference to me what my father says. I'm a man and able to choose my own wife." He looked at his father. "We are going now," he said firmly.

There was no reply.

The door closed behind his son. John Boland staggered to a couch and falling down beside it buried his face in his arms.

CHAPTER XXV

THE INTERESTS VERSUS MARY RANDALL

If John Boland was shaken by the interview with his son, there was no evidence of it in his bearing when he appeared at the offices of the Electric Trust the following morning. As he took his accustomed place at his desk he looked tired, but he wore what La Salle street knew as his fighting face.

Boland had scarcely established himself for the day when he discovered that his decision to remain in Chicago had been anticipated by those who knew him well in affairs. A dozen messages were waiting for him. The forces opposed to Mary Randall and her reforms looked to him for leadership.

As soon as the details of the raid on the Cafe Sinister had become definitely known, there had been a quick general movement on the part of the leaders of the Levee to get together. They met in secret places to deplore the taking off of Anson, to form alliances against their common enemy. From these meetings went appeals for protection to the forces higher up.

Aid was invoked of the great financial interests involved, directly and indirectly, in the traffic in souls. Political overlords of the city sent word that the protection demanded should not be wanting. Within twelve hours they had effected an organization whose ramifications extended into wholly unexpected places. Then, having formed the machine, they turned with one accord to John Boland to guide it.

His acceptance of this leadership was unavoidable, even if he had wished to avoid it. To reject it would have been treason to the forces which had fought side by side with him in many a former and desperate campaign. To give Boland credit, his courage was equal to the task he had no wish to avoid. He knew the situation was dangerous, but he was a fighter born.

Having made up his mind to give battle, Boland addressed himself to the task of outlining his campaign. He was too shrewd, too thoroughly familiar with all the elements making up Chicago, to underestimate his enemy. He knew that Mary Randall was appealing passionately to a public morality which hated the vice system with a wholehearted hatred. He knew, too, that when the light of truth fell upon his followers they would scurry to shelter. His first step was to exclude from his offices every employe of whose loyalty he could not be completely certain. He had his bitter lesson on that score, certainly, he told himself.

By telephone and by private messenger he proceeded to summon his chief allies to a conference. These men arrived within an hour. One was a United States Senator, two were bankers of impeccable reputation. One was a political boss whose authority was a by-word in one of the great parties, another a philanthropist whose spectacular gratuities to public institutions came from huge dividends made for him by underpaid employes, and with him a clergyman managed by this philanthropist and the bankers and a newspaper publisher whose little soul had been often bought and sold, so that certain of his profession were wont to say one could see thumb-marks of Mammon on him as he passed by.

Boland did not invite Grogan to this meeting. He intended at first to ask him, but his friend had shown too much sympathy of late with sentiment in life.

John Boland's council of war was in session for five hours. Every phase of the situation was taken up and discussed with thoroughness characteristic of these leaders of men, with thoroughness, too, that showed full familiarity with all the conditions of commercialized vice in Chicago. The evasions and bombast wherewith these citizens were accustomed to adorn their public addresses before vice commission inquiries were strangely lacking. They spoke among themselves plainly and without pretenses.

Towards the close of this conference John Boland offered his plan of action:

"Gentlemen," he addressed the others from the head of his directors' table in his inner office. "We all agree that what we have most to fear is publicity. In fact, if these reformers had no publicity they would be without weapons. As you are aware, the extent to which we can control the newspapers is limited. If news comes to them in the regular way they are bound to print it, so if we are to avoid disastrous publicity we must stop it at its source.

"At this moment the 'news' of the situation centers about Druce and those of his employes who are now in jail. We can't prevent his being indicted, we can't prevent his case coming to trial, if we allow him to remain in jail.

"My friends, I need not tell you that such a trial would fill the newspapers with what they call 'exposures' of vice conditions that would be calamitous. You all agree with me that vice is a terrible thing. We know—none better, as our discussions have indicated—how great this evil is in our city.

But there is something more menacing than vice,—namely, an ill-controlled and hysterical anti-vice crusade, rushing on and intoxicating itself with its own sensations, and shaking the business fabric of the city.

"Think of the want that will come to the poor in Chicago if confidence in our leading business men should be seriously shaken! It is our duty as pillars—if I may say so—of Chicago's financial structure to avoid, to prevent, public trials of vice cases.

"How are we to go about suppressing the excitement of a trial of Martin Druce? Various expedients suggest themselves to us all. Is not the most feasible to have Druce released on bail?"

"Yes, to any amount!" called two voices.

"I believe the matter can be arranged," replied John Boland, graciously. "Indeed, I have taken the liberty to discuss that phase of the situation with Judge Grundell. He is of opinion that Druce can be freed. My own attorneys have given the subject some consideration also. As I understand it, Druce is booked for murder—"

"Is murder a bailable offense in Chicago?"

"Ordinarily, no. But in this case it can be shown that there were extenuating circumstances. We can make a showing of facts to demonstrate that the killing of Carter Anson was purely accidental."

"Druce was only trying to shoot Mary Randall, as I heard it," said a grim voice.

"H'm! Suppose we say instead that Druce thought some one

was creating a disturbance in his place of business, became excited and fired. The bullet hit Anson. Our opponents are not expecting, probably, any move by us towards the release of Druce on bail. It is unlikely that they will resist the application. In any event, I have already taken up the matter with the judge.

"With Druce freed and resting in safe seclusion, I consider it advisable to place him in possession of facilities that will enable him to remain at liberty for an indefinite period— until this excitement has blown over, you understand."

"We can send him out to China on business," said one.

"Exactly. My attorney has a young man who will see that he is rightly started on his journey, avoiding all publicity. The cases of his employes will come on for trial; but with Druce out of the way, it will be extremely difficult for our opponents to obtain any convictions. Thus this whole sensation will fall flat and the reform crusaders will find themselves discredited before the public."

Applause welcomed John Boland's summing up of the situation and his formulation of a practical plan. Members of the conference rose smiling cheerfully, shook hands all around and made it plain that each was ready to pay, pay, pay. The door had not closed behind them before John Boland set in motion the machinery which was to set Martin Druce free.

CHAPTER XXVI

OUT ON BAIL

When Martin Druce heard the news that bail had been raised for his release and that all arrangements were being made for his flight and concealment, it was exactly half an hour before the bail bond was signed and the order sent to the prison that he should be set at liberty.

Broken by his incarceration, terrified by his murderous experience of the last night at the cafe, red-eyed and restless, the dive-keeper was pacing up and down his cell. A pick-pocket whom he knew and who, through his own political pull was serving a term as a trusty, brought the information to him scrawled on a bit of cigarette paper which, with a little warning whistle, he dropped through the bars of the steel cage.

Druce picked up the note and read it furtively. He waited for the trusty to pass him again, then beckoning him, he whispered, "See if my gal isn't outside somewhere. She just left here. Tell her to wait. She can get into the automobile which they will be sure to send for me."

It was not affection, but cowardice, that led Druce to think of Elsie first. Since he had been locked up he had crumbled under his trouble. He was so much shaken in mind and body by the killing of Anson and by his arrest that he was actually afraid to go out of the jail alone.

After what seemed an eternity of waiting he heard footsteps in the corridor. A guard appeared and unlocked the iron door, beckoned to Druce, and he passed out.

In a little waiting-room an iron-faced jail attendant handed him his watch and knife and some money taken from him when he was locked up. A lawyer whom he knew signaled him to follow.

Another steel door stood open and Druce found himself outside the prison, breathing the free air of night. An automobile stood there. Druce saw that Elsie was already within.

"The driver has instructions," said the lawyer. "Later you will hear further from me."

"What to hell are they going to do for me?" growled Druce.

"No time to argue," said the lawyer. "Here!" He pressed something in his hand. "Your game is to get away while the getting is good." He slammed the door as Druce got in. The car turned the corner and went north.

"Where are we going?" Elsie asked.

Druce mumbled an unintelligible answer.

"Where?"

"Shut up your ranting at me!" He shook off her hand. "I guess you'll get your three squares a day."

Nothing more was said for several moments. Elsie lay back with her eyes closed. By the light from occasional street lamps Druce was counting a roll of bills.

"Here, kid, look at this." He spoke with just a touch of softness and bravado. "That young guy slipped it to me. My backers got to give me a nice trip to foreign lands. There'll be plenty of kale. I'm going to take you along, see." He did not add that her too great knowledge of his methods made others desirous that she, too, should be far away when the trial of the dive's employes came to pass. Elsie opened her eyes.

"I should think you would show that you feel a little bit glad that I'm out," he whined. "Think of those days in that jail."

Elsie would not have dared fail to express sympathy for him, but he was in need of a match for the cigarette he held. Hailing the chauffeur, he had the next instant forgotten his demand.

They drove in silence until they reached the house that had been prepared for their hiding-place. "Furnished rooms— Light Housekeeping" was inscribed on a card, tacked conspicuously in the doorway.

A woman near middle age, inclined to be fleshy, with large features that reflected the dim hall light, met them, her arms akimbo.

"Everything's all right for you folks. Upstairs front. There's a gas stove in the closet if you all—

"We ain't pikers—we'll get our eats sent in. Here, take this." Druce put a slip of paper and a greenback into Elsie's hand.

"Go to the drug-store there at the corner and get this

prescription filled," he ordered. "It's morphine. I've got to sleep tonight."

Elsie obeyed passively. When she returned Druce was pacing the room wild with impatience. His greenbacks and a bottle of absinthe lay on the table.

He lost no time in resorting to the morphine. "Absinthe is the stuff to put life in your body; but it's the good old dope to make you forget all your troubles," he soliloquized, Very shortly he was on the bed, sound asleep.

Elsie paced softly back and forth in the room for a long time. Then she went out into the dark hallway. She opened the window and stood looking into the street. It was quiet there. The stars looked down on a deserted way.

That big bright star over there! Was it not the one she and her sister used to choose when wishing from their bedroom window at Millville! How long ago that seemed; how wide and dreadful life's abyss between!

"If I had known, if I had known!" Elsie shuddered and glanced towards the closed door. "I was bound to have my own way. My—own—way. That's it. There was something in me—" She faced her actions, she probed into her thoughts from the hour she first met Martin Druce. She marshalled her scathing shames before the judgment bar of her womanhood. In the flaming fires of tortured conscience she stood and suffered.

Then she began to wonder about the future. Where was she bound? Where would he be sent? What strange lands might she see?

How could she go with him? How could she stay behind?

The street—the dreadful streets of night!

Elsie shuddered, remembering those nights in the Levee, the fear and horror, and at last the shameful, gnawing hunger that drove her to him again.

Back in the room where the dive-keeper lay in stupor Elsie spread a quilt on the floor and went wearily to her broken rest.

When she awoke Druce was trying nervously to roll a cigarette. The paper broke.

"Here, you, it's morning. It's time you woke up. Take this money. Get me some cigarettes. I can't roll them."

He was a being frightening to see by this time. The morphine and the French poison had torn his nerves to fragments. His eyes glared like coals in his pasty white face.

Elsie did not try to talk to him. She saw that he was beyond that. She took some money from the table and went out again to buy the cigarettes and food. When she returned Druce refused to eat. He took up the bottle of absinthe and drank from it, swallowing the burning liquid with animal-like gulps that made Elsie shudder.

"You'll kill yourself," said Elsie. "Take some of this milk."

"Mind your own damn business," returned Druce, hoarsely. "You stick to milk. I'll stick to absinthe."

Again he lay down and again he slept. The long day passed. Night came and with a wild wind and a beating rain.

Druce woke in a half delirium.

"More absinthe, more absinthe," he muttered. The bottle on the table was empty. "Why didn't you have another bottle here? What have you been doing, eh?"

"Do you think you better take any more?" asked Elsie.

Druce stood glaring at her. His eyes flamed as he rushed across the room like a madman. Before she could get out of his way he struck her a brutal blow that felled her to the floor, and kicked her as she struggled. He reached for the empty bottle and brandished it over her.

"Damn you, get out of here quick and get me that dope!"

Elsie got to her feet.

"I'll go," she said, faintly.

CHAPTER XXVII

HARVEY SPENCER TAKES UP THE TRAIL

Harvey had waited about the jail for days. He was certain that Elsie Welcome would return to Druce, and he was resolved to make a great effort to induce her to leave him.

In his unsubtle makeup the measure of his devotion was as great as the measure of his unspoiled manhood. The girl he wished to make his wife had been taken from him. She had removed herself far from his kindness and care, but he could not cease to offer her the care she needed more poignantly than before.

The personal interest of so conspicuous a person as Mary Randall, in Elsie's case, had undoubtedly urged Harvey on— when otherwise he might have given up. Even so, his courage and persistency, and personal sacrifices, were wonderful to behold.

On the night when Druce was at last removed from the jail Harvey was standing in an alley opposite the public entrance to the jail watching the automobile which stood awaiting the coming of someone from within.

Finally he saw the slender figure of a woman emerge from a

Virginia Brooks

doorway and enter the automobile. He knew that figure. He ran across the street and around the car. He noted its number with one of those keen flashes of memory, conscious at the moment that he should remember that number as long as he drew breath.

He flung open the door on the further side of the automobile.

Elsie faced him. "What are you doing here?" she asked in an icy little voice.

"I—no—Won't you come to your mother, Elsie? Won't you come away from this man? Your mother and Patience love you so much and have been trying so hard to find you and—"

"I can't, Harvey—I—perhaps—Oh! Go away. Druce is coming. He will—hurt you."

"It doesn't matter about me. It's you."

"I—I must stand by my husband."

"Husband! He isn't your husband. He fooled you with a marriage license. Anybody can get a license in Chicago, but Druce's license was never returned. He likely got some fellow to pretend to perform the marriage. Elsie, it wasn't legal, I can prove it."

For an instant Elsie's spirit flamed in her eyes and her burning cheeks paled. Then she saw Druce coming and she turned towards him wearily, a strange quivering and drooping of her eyelids alone showing that she had heard. In the presence of her master she grew meek as a little child.

Harvey drifted back into the shadows of the jail, powerless to help her, and saw her driven away with the man who had ruined her earthly life.

Fighting his grief and despair, he went to the nearest drug-store and telephoned Miss Randall of what he had seen.

"Druce out on bail! A murderer out on bail in Chicago!" she exclaimed. "Oh, Harvey, if only you had thought to jump into a taxicab and follow them to see where they have been taken."

"I'm no detective. I am going back to Millville. Perhaps I can get back my old job in the grocery store," he answered grimly.

"Hello! Miss Randall! Hello! I remember the number of the machine." He gave it.

"Good! Wait a minute till I see whose that is. Hold the wire." She consulted her list of the automobile numbers entered in Illinois and found that this one belonged to a professional bondsman named Comstock.

She gave Harvey the man's residence number.

"Go out there first thing in the morning and see if you can find out from the chauffeur where the machine went tonight. Keep a stiff upper lip, Mr. Spencer, you have really done splendidly."

Harvey went early next day to the address given him, a residence of the type called stone-fronted, in a district no longer fashionable. There was a garage, but no automobile. Harvey made a careful survey of the premises without gaining ground. He saw another of Mary Randall's aids come, linger about and go away; but remembering her advice about keeping a stiff upper lip, he stayed on. He was to be rewarded late in the afternoon.

A car rumbled into the garage. Its colored driver immediately began washing it and Harvey sauntered back into the yard. The number on it was the one printed on his memory.

From somewhere back in his tired brain came the impulse to say,

"I'm a repair man from Gavin's garage. Mr. Comstock told me to come over and take a look at his car. Said he had it out in the rain last night and it wasn't working right."

"Yes, sah; that car certainly has been drove last night. Some of the battery connections got wet." The chauffeur was glib enough.

"Lights and ignition out of order?" Harvey pretended to examine the car, asking seemingly careless questions and gaining from the negro the information that the car had gone from the jail with Druce to an obscure street far out on the northwest side. The man could not give the number of the house, but said it was one of three in the middle of "a short little street."

Harvey made the excuse that he must go back to the garage where he was employed to get his tools, and hurried away.

It was growing dark and a wild, stormy rain-wind was blowing when he reached the remote neighborhood described for him by the bondsman's talkative servant. He was gazing at the three forbidding dwellings standing near the center of the block, trying to make up his mind which to approach first, when he saw Elsie in her long rain-coat come out of the middle house, hesitate a moment, then hurry down the steps into the street.

He slipped into the shadow of a house, his heart thumping.

"Elsie!" he called softly in a voice scarcely above a whisper.

She stopped, startled.

"Is it Harvey?" Elsie peered doubtingly into the darkness, then stepped trustingly towards him as he replied,

"Yes, it's sure Harvey." He caught the sadness in her words and his voice shook. "Won't you come away with me now? Your mother wants you!"

"Your life is in danger with him. Why don't you leave him?" he added earnestly.

"Leave him," she repeated. "Oh, if I only could! My mother and Patience—how are they?"

"They are well and safe, only they want you. They're going back to Millville, to the same cottage. It's going to be all fixed over. Patience is going to be married—Mr. Harry Boland."

Tears streamed from Elsie's eyes. She leaned against the iron fence that skirted the sidewalk.

"Don't you see, Harvey, I just couldn't go home? I couldn't bear to make Patience—ashamed of me. Don't tell her that, though, will you? Tell them that I have to stay with my—my—oh, don't let mother know you saw me. Don't let her know any different."

"You poor little thing—"

She looked about her in alarm. "I mustn't stay here. You

mustn't, either. It's no use, Harvey. The life's got me—I can't turn back."

The next moment she was running down the street as if hurrying from a pursuer.

Harvey saw her enter the corner drug-store, waited a little while, then decided he too had business in the drug-store. He would telephone Miss Randall—but he must be careful. Elsie was receiving a package from the drug clerk, as he entered the 'phone booth—and left while he was talking. Harvey was standing with his face to the wall, speaking in a whisper, lest his message would be overheard. He did not see Elsie depart.

He got the reformer herself on the telephone.

"I have found them," he said.

"Good!" Joy and relief were in her tones. "Watch them carefully, won't you? We'll have detectives there in a jiffy with a new warrant for Druce. This time for white slavery. He will not escape us again."

Harvey gave the number of the house where Druce and Elsie had been hidden, appointed a rendezvous with the detective and returned at once to watch the house. He decided that Elsie had hurried back while he was at the telephone.

In less than an hour an automobile rushed up to the house. Two men got out and hurried into the place. One of them he recognized as the lawyer he had seen at the entrance of the jail. There were not his detectives.

The storm had increased and the rain was driving in blinding torrents across the street.

Harvey saw a group of people suddenly emerge from the house. The chauffeur jumped down and took part with the struggling little crowd. He could hear Druce swearing loudly, calling out Elsie's name with words of abuse. The men pushed the drunken man into the car, and got in after him.

Harvey looked about for some sort of a vehicle, but none was in sight and the auto was actually starting. He sprang on the rear, spring and, crouching, hung on desperately. They drove for a long time; to him it seemed hours as his hands grew numb and his muscles ached from clinging to his precarious hold. Fortunately the storm had subsided.

The driver turned into a dark, cobble paved street. The auto swayed and jolted like a ship on the rocks. The road was full of pitch-holes and as the wheels slipped into them a blinding spray of muddy water was flung into Harvey's face. The machine put on more speed and swung around a corner. Another hole! The car careened, almost turned over, and Harvey was thrown into the street.

As he struggled to his feet the red rear light of the automobile was two blocks away. But he went on, gasping for breath, stumbling. Presently he found himself in the district near the river, close to the north side water front, which is deserted after night-fall.

He had hurried on like a man in a dream. Now he came to the edge of the river and stood staring down into the water.

Out in the stream he could see the shadowy outline of a boat. Looking more closely, he saw that he was scarcely two hundred feet from the craft. The darkness had multiplied the distance; it was now penetrated by a lantern light moving on the deck, evidently in the hand of someone who was standing aft on the boat.

There was distinct, loud talking and swearing between men.

Harvey thought that it was a fishing smack. Its demonstrative passengers were bent upon waking up the night and almost woke him up to the purpose of his night's errand when he heard a loud voice say:

"Cut that out, Druce. No more boozing, d'you hear?"

"D-r-u-c-e."

Harvey was as near fainting as a healthy young man might be with the shock of this surprise after his tremendous exertions and his fall. He stood as if petrified.

But his ears still caught the sound of swearing and he saw men moving quickly about on the deck, then the gray white of sails spreading like gaunt ghosts. The swish of water told him that the boat was moving, that his quarry was slipping into pitch-blackness ahead.

That was the finish of his courage.

Harvey felt his limbs trembling, felt something trickle down his face. He was beaten.

CHAPTER XXVIII

THE FORCES THAT CONQUER

When the tenderloin learned that Martin Druce had been released on a bond for thirty thousand dollars, the tenderloin laughed.

The laugh was low and cunning and there was more than the suggestion of a sneer in it. It rang from one end of the district to the other, convulsing dive-keepers who for days had been as funereal as undertakers. It sounded in dance halls and bagnios, in barrooms and gambling dens.

It eddied up into Chicago's higher air and found an echo in clubs frequented by distinguished financier-politicians.

John Boland had won! The brain that had never failed had proved its resourcefulness once again in this hour of dire trouble. Druce was gone. He would never be heard of in Chicago again. It had cost thirty thousand dollars, but what was thirty thousand dollars? Mary Randall and her crusaders were crushed. Anson was dead. Druce was gone.

What mattered it now how much evidence Mary Randall had gathered in against the Cafe Sinister! There would be a period of quiet. The tenderloin would carefully observe all the proprieties. Then the case of the State against Martin Druce would be called and Druce would not respond to that summons. And so Mary Randall's sensation would die an unnatural death—death from smothering, death from lack of expression. Afterward the tenderloin would resume its old operations. No wonder the tenderloin laughed!

John Boland felt none of this exultation when he returned to his office on the morning following Druce's release. An indefinable oppression weighed him down. He had won, he knew—and yet the air about him seemed charged with prescience of evil. He tried to shake it off and could not. He was anxious, too, about Harry. Why, he asked himself, should he worry about an ungrateful son. John Boland did not know the answer, yet the answer was very plain. His son Harry was his own flesh and blood and no man can cut himself off from his own flesh and blood without feeling some sort of reaction.

John Boland, the man of brain and iron was only human after all. He loved his son.

He was in a state of gloomy meditation when he opened his desk and resumed his day's work. The telephone bell jangled constantly. The councillors who had participated in the conference over Druce's case which had resulted so happily were calling up to congratulate Boland on the success of his maneuver. Somehow these felicitations did not please him as his fellow advisers had expected.

His mood was gloomy. He could not shake it off. Constantly the same question returned to his mind he had won, yes, but what difference did it make? Was he any happier? Was the world any better? Boland had never been worried by questions of this sort before. He could not answer them.

He was still in this gray mood when the guardian of his door announced the arrival of Grogan. Michael Grogan was, perhaps, Boland's most intimate friend. He had not taken Grogan into his confidence when he planned his coup to release Druce. He felt that Grogan would not be in sympathy with his campaign for destroying the work of the reformers. Still he was glad to see Grogan. After all he was a friend. And this morning John Boland, for the first time, perhaps, in his life, felt the need of a friend.

"John," said Grogan taking a seat, "I see you've 'sprung' Druce?"

"Yes? Mike you're an inveterate reader of the newspapers."

"They're yelling about it this morning."

"Let them yell."

"You did it?"

"Well Mike, I'm a modest man. I had something to do with it."

"It's a rotten business!"

"What!"

"I said it was a rotten business."

"The commercial interests of the city demanded it. Do you think I will stand idly by and see a bunch of half-baked reformers shake down the business institutions of Chicago?"

"John, they are right."

"O yes, I suppose if you take the mamby-pamby, hysterical, sentimental end of it, any campaign that hits at vice is right."

"It was a great movement. Mary Randall is a fine girl. You'll live to regret that you helped to thwart her."

"Pshaw, what's the matter with you, man? You're blood seems to be turning to milk. The papers will howl for a few days and then they'll forget it. We'll invite them to. We'll suggest that if they don't forget it the interests we represent may feel called upon to cut down their advertising. They'll forget it all right."

"No, John," Grogan spoke deliberately. "You can't kill off a great and righteous movement by choking a few newspapers. The newspapers are powerful but their power has its limits. That girl has built a fire under this town that will rage in spite of you or me, or any one else. We can't stop it." Grogan rose. "That's all," he said, "I just dropped in to let you know how I feel about it. I thought I might be able to persuade you to get out of this fight. I guess, John, you're incorrigible. Well, no hard feelings."

Boland laughed. "Have a drink as you go out. You need something to cheer you up."

Grogan stopped. "Where's Harry?" he asked suddenly.

Boland flushed and his brow darkened.

"I don't know," he answered. "He and I have had a mis-understanding. He insists on marrying this Welcome girl. I don't know where he is and I don't care."

Grogan looked surprised. "John," he said, "I'd feel sorry for you if I didn't know you are lying. You do care. You can't conceal it. You care now, and worse you'll be caring more and more as time goes on. John, there are some things even you can't do."

"Well, Mike, what are they?"

"You can't beat Nature and you can't beat God. Good day."

In vain Boland scoffed at Grogan's sentimentalism. Again and again the words rose in his mind:

You can't beat Nature and you can't beat God.

The telephone rang. At the other end of the wire was that senator who had been at his conference. He asked Boland in a frightened voice if he had seen the papers, and then rang off.

Boland, alarmed, sent a boy in haste for the latest editions. The boy returned and spread them out on the desk before him.

Again the telephone rang. This time it was the clergyman who had participated in the conference.

"Do you know that Mary Randall is out in a statement that she knows full details of what she calls the plot that resulted in the liberation of Martin Druce?" he demanded. "She says she will give the whole thing to the newspapers later. They are calling it in the streets below my study window now. Can't something be done to head off that statement?"

"What would you suggest? Why don't you see some of the editors?" Boland returned.

"Oh, that's impossible. My dear Boland, think of me. If my

name should be published in this connection my reputation would be ruined."

Boland laughed savagely into the telephone and hung up the receiver, only to lift it again and hear another appeal for help, this from the publisher. He also feared ruin.

Another call. The politician whose power in a great political party was a by-word was barking at the other end of the wire. He accused Boland of destroying him.

"You've destroyed us," he yelped. "We're ruined. You've blundered."

Boland was beyond speech by this time. He seized his hat and rushed out into the street. Everywhere boys were shouting the extras. Several people who recognized him as he passed paused to look after him curiously. He walked directly to his club.

A few men gathered there reading newspapers paused to look after him curiously, bowed coldly and at once resumed reading. Others seemed to avoid him. Boland felt that the newspapers' conspicuous comment on a certain financial magnate prominent in the electrical world in connection with the vice-scandal pointed at him too plainly for any one in Chicago to misunderstand.

He called his car and drove to his lonely home.

That night John Boland had a strange vision. He saw an eternity of pain and everlasting darkness. Through it the nightmare of his past life in strangely terrifying pictures passed before his mind.

Scenes of his boyhood, the panorama of his young manhood,

pictures of his battle for success against overwhelming forces in the great city. These pictures returned again and again, vivid in their relief. He saw again the death of his wife and the spirit of darkness that had then come to walk beside him, taunting him that now he was of necessity a cold, calculating, lonely, indomitable man, not knowing how to give to his only son fatherly tenderness.

This phase passed. He seemed to enter into a larger world full of terrifying monsters, all of human form. One he recognized as Druce, another as Anson, a third as the senator whose seat he had helped to get. And with them came a host of smaller figures, some struggling for life, and being crushed down into oblivion under his inexorable progress, some fighting with one another lest they too be torn down and crushed before him.

There were piteous girl faces and worn kindly faces of women and men and these had gone down before the others because they had not the power of resistance needed in this battle. It was a great whirling nightmare of continuous struggle.

And always walking by his side and seeming to grow stronger and more terrible as he tore his path through every obstacle strode his guide, the spirit of darkness.

At last they were alone, he and the spirit. And the spirit turned upon him and clutched him by the throat. He struggled in that grasp just as others had struggled in his own grasp, tortured and futile. And again those words from Grogan:

"You can't beat Nature and you can't beat God!"

Sweat stood out on John Boland's forehead.

He awoke with a mighty effort and sat upright. Around him was the emptiness and loneliness of the great bed-chamber. He saw with eyes wide open and brain alert a picture that looked like a reality and not a vision.

It was of a trembling man bent with age and loneliness.

CHAPTER XXIX

THE CALL OF ETERNITY

Elsie walked on and on eastward towards the lake. For a week she had been living alone in a room she had found near the park on the night that she left Harvey Spencer, telephoning in the drug-store. She had resolved that instant to go. It was to be "Now or never"—and she hurried away in an opposite direction from the hiding place—and from Druce.

The little money that he had put in her hands for drugs had somehow lasted her until now. She had been too ill to go out, her body racked with fever.

She was conscious that she must tomorrow find some work to do, for the landlady had twice asked her for the next week's rent. She looked in at the door of a laundry where a German woman was singing as she ironed children's dresses by the light of a flaring gas jet. It looked pleasant and peaceful in there. Perhaps that motherly woman would let her work with her. She would see tomorrow.

Elsie walked on towards the lake. She wanted to look at the water. She wanted to breathe the cool breath of great winds coming over the water to cool this fierce fire of shame and horror fevering her soul, flaming in her delicate cheeks.

Elsie came to the lake front at a wide high lot between two comfortable mansions on Sheridan Road.

Lights of homes shone through the night's darkness. Beams as of sunshine danced across the water.

A light from an upper chamber in the nearest home shone across her and streamed onward to the sands.

Elsie stood clasping and unclasping her little slender hands. The waters,—they could wash away that blow, the marks of that blow, wash away those words threatening death from one who had killed something in her heart. She realized that she was not afraid, facing the life to come.

She was afraid only to go on living in the same world with one who had taken her girlhood and her womanhood, afraid only of this frightful fever in her veins, of this poison that was consuming her.

Out yonder were the cool deeps of death—of death? What then? Far across the waves she saw a light.

It was as if her spirit went to meet the light, went in quest of the meaning of such a beacon light across black waters.

The light seemed to grow bigger and bigger as she gazed. By flinging her frail body into the dreadful surges could one reach peace and safety?

Faintly her spirit heard the answer of the pursuing hound of heaven, faintly she heard the call of eternity and of the Eternal Love.

The great black billows called to her. Elsie wondered what all the poor girls the waves toss up along the shores say to their Maker. She seemed to feel with them as she stood there, how the waves seize the bodies of the lost,—how the undertow takes them. Elsie put her hands to her face.

"Why am I here alone in the night?" she heard herself asking. Her voice sounded strangely familiar, yet unfamiliar as if some one were speaking to her. Then she knew that the voice was her own soul in the silence.

"Mother will forgive me, mother wants me back, mother will help me get well—if there is any health in me. Mother knows that it wasn't all my fault—" her thought defended her against that voice.

"Why am I here alone in the night?" the question was repeated.

"I will go home. I will begin again. Men begin again. Oh!..." A sob came from her lips.... "No, no, no!"

She felt with every nerve of her quivering being that in the slow upward climb of sex towards true love and true parenthood woman's battle is man's,—felt that God and Nature are now demanding not less of men.

The suffering girl could not put her certainty into words, but in her body and in her soul she knew—she knew.

Suddenly from the opened window of the nearest home she heard above the wind the cry of a baby, the loud, sweet, prolonged, fiercely-demanding cry of a hungry little baby.

A wistful smile twisted her lips as she listened.

Suddenly as the baby's cry was stopped she put her hands to her bosom and a strange lovely light shone on her face.

CHAPTER XXX

AT THE WEDDING FEAST

Brightly shone the sunshine on the fields and woods surrounding Millville and on the little house where Mrs. Welcome was busy putting the last touches to the order and sweetness of home.

Patience and her husband were coming on the noon train.

Later in the day a few of their friends had promised to come to the supper for which her mother had been making loaves of delicious cake.

"It is strange, strange that my child should be the wife of John Boland's son," she mused. "I wonder what my poor man would say. Would he feel less bitter if he could know that Boland sent me all that money, with that letter 'as justice to Tom Welcome's widow?' Patience and Harry are so happy now it makes me feel like wanting to forget the past. If only I could know where my baby girl is. But I just must go on trusting. Somehow I feel hopeful. Patience and Harry want me to be brave. Harry's father—he must find it hard to be brave too. He must be lonesome, estranged from his son, no one to comfort him. Perhaps he sent me that money really as a sign to Harry that he wants to be friends again. I won't say anything to Harry about it just yet, but maybe some of these days...." The direct train of her thought was interrupted by the sound of a bird singing on the bough of a tree close by the opened window.

She stepped out into the side porch and looked about her with a glance of pleasure in the neatness and charm of the little place. House and fence had been painted and mended, put in tidy order. A new gate and a cement sidewalk in front running down to the corner of the street spoke for the industry of Harvey Spencer who had worked like a son for her in his spare hours.

The song of the bird in the elm bough had dropped to a happy twittering. The fragrance of late garden blossoms filled the air. At the end of the deep yard, beyond the vegetable garden and close to the back gate Harvey had built a pretty summer house and over it a madeira vine hung its abundant quick growing wreaths of green.

Mrs. Welcome in her light summer dress, her gray hair moved a trifle by the soft warm breeze, walked slowly down the garden path and sat down for a few moments of rest in this quiet spot. A sudden sadness came upon her face as almost always these months since her home coming when she rested from her working.

But she rose resolutely and banished the thought.

"Today is my oldest daughter's day. I must think of nobody but Patience and make her coming home with her husband as glad as can be."

She spoke aloud, to make her resolution stronger and walked back towards the house, gathering nasturtiums and asparagus as she went, to decorate the fresh and pretty parlor, with its new white muslin curtains and wall paper and the piano which Harry Boland had sent.

"It's perfectly lovely, mother," Patience was saying to her in this room within the hour, Patience whom everybody in Millville loved, standing radiant and happy beside her equally radiant bridegroom. "How did you ever get those flowers to trail over that picture as if they just grew there?"

"You're a great success as a decorator, and we can't begin to thank you enough," said Harry Boland. "I think Patience and I are in great luck that we can make our home with you. It's all settled that I'm to have that office opposite the court-house, going to buy and sell real estate and work up a regular business."

"Yes, and mother, Harry finds that a whole lot of these cottages the mill people live in are really his own, from his mother's estate directly to him. He's going to put them all in decent order."

"Do you remember Michael Grogan? He is going to help us do things in Millville. He has promised to build us a club house and dance hall, a social center for the mill young people if you and Patience will help run it."

"That's fine. Young folks need their fun," responded Mrs. Welcome heartily. "Come along, Patey dear, and see the cakes mother has been baking for you and Harry."

Mary Randall and Michael Grogan, Harvey Spencer and his sister and brother-in-law were the five guests who assembled in the late afternoon to honor the home-coming of Mr. and Mrs. Harry Boland.

Michael Grogan came first, arriving in a carriage of the hack type from the station. He brought a huge bouquet of roses for the bride and a case of grape-juice for the cheer of the festivity.

At supper he proposed the health of the young pair.

"May they always live happy ever after," said Grogan, standing up, glass in hand. "May they never have any troubles that they can't nip in the bud. As their principles demand of 'em to drink this stuff as the pure juice of the grape, may it be blessed to 'em forever and to their descendants."

Every body laughed and drank. Harry Boland toasted him in return:

"Here's the health of our very good friend, Mr. Michael Grogan. May all his mornings be golden and all his sunsets clear."

"Thanks for the sunrises in particular," said Grogan. "Now ladies and gentlemen I wish to toast the good health of another young lady who is with us today, one who has made me a great deal of trouble and scared me blue with blue envelopes. May she soon find a bridegroom for herself, one of them brave lads who can talk right back to her as I never could when she tackled this old man!" He lifted his grape-juice with a great flourish. "Here's to herself, Miss Mary Randall!"

Miss Randall blushed and nodded her thanks.

"Speech, speech," demanded Grogan.

"Thank you, thank you but I just can't, not here, not now," she said and quiet fell upon them.

The thoughts of all were with the young girl who had disappeared, for whom all had worked, suffered, prayed.

"I do want to say," Miss Randall, broke the silence, "that you all must know how glad I am that Mr. and Mrs. Harry Boland are to have a useful and happy life together and that I...." She stopped suddenly, looking out the opened door that led towards the garden, her whole expression changing, her lips parting, her breath coming quickly.

"What did you see out there?" asked Harvey Spencer, with the sharp intentness which he had learned from his maturing city experience.

"Now constable, don't get excited," chaffed Grogan, to whose aid Harvey's quick rise to prominence and office was in part due. "We don't want to be catching any burglars this happy day."

"What is it?" asked Patience Boland, rising.

"I—I don't know, to be really certain." Mary looked at Mrs. Welcome. "Somebody came in at the back gate and went into the summer-house."

Mrs. Welcome leaned heavily on the table.

Harvey ran to the window. Grogan looked over his shoulder.

"Oh, Miss Randall, please go out and see." Patience's arms were already about her mother. "Mumsey, mumsey, can it be?"

Mary went out into the porch and down the garden path.

It was Elsie Welcome who came out of the summer-house

and slowly along between the flower borders. She was shockingly emaciated. She stopped and put her suit case down on the ground; its weight seemed too great for her spent strength.

Mary ran to her.

Elsie looked at her with sorrowful dark eyes.

"I am afraid to go in," she said.

"I hear people in there talking and laughing."

"They are all friends of yours."

"Is my mother—will my mother...?"

"Child, your mother's heart is breaking for the sight of you."

Elsie ran forward to the doorway of the familiar room. A step forward. Mother and daughter stood in a tender embrace.

The mother's face was radiant with great warmth of love. Patience rushed to her sister and clasped her close.

Michael Grogan had led a tiptoe retreat of the visitors leaving mother and daughters alone, but Patience called them back.

Elsie, smiling wanly, slipped like a little wraith across and into a chair beside her mother, and felt that dear hand clasping hers.

"It's so good to be here with you," she whispered, looking vaguely about at the others, then a dreadful fit of coughing seized her and she sank exhausted in her mother's arms.

Harvey helped carry her into the little room off the parlor.

"You dear little thing, all you need is lots of fresh eggs and your ma's nursing to set you up again," he said to her.

"Yes, Harvey, she is feeling very ill now, but we will all help her get well," said Patience, as they went out of the room together, leaving Elsie to rest in her mother's care.

CHAPTER XXXI

WITH THE ROSES OF LOVE

Mrs. Welcome came into the little bedroom very quietly one afternoon about a week later, in her hands a large glass bowl overflowing with roses.

She put it down on the table beside the bed and stood looking wistfully at the small dark head on the pillow.

Elsie felt her there, opened her eyes and smiled as she saw the flowers. A deeper color burned for a moment in her cheeks.

"Poor Harvey," she said. "Isn't he a dear, mamma?"

"He always thought the world and all of you," Mrs. Welcome sighed.

"I always liked him, but I never did love him, you know. I just let him come to see me because he wanted to, and all the girls had company."

"You might have loved him dearie if—if—"

"If I hadn't gone away, you mean, but I did go away." Elsie

coughed violently.

"There, there, sweet, don't." Her mother helped her to sit up and held her in her arms.

"Harvey comes every day to ask how you are," said Mrs. Welcome when she was better. "He wants to see you when you feel able."

Elsie remained silent.

Out in the parlor they could hear Patience moving about, putting things in order, singing as she worked one of the songs she and Elsie used to sing when they were little girls.

"Young Mrs. Boland is some singer," said Elsie with a flash of her old fun. "Isn't it nice for our Patey to be so happy?"

"She and I want you to be happy too, and you will when you get well, my precious. You will laugh and sing as you used to."

"Mamma, I see through you," said Elsie. "I bet Harvey is here now. He brought these roses himself. He coaxed you to coax me to see him. All right. Shake up my pillows. Get Patey's pink boudoir cap and put your pink shawl around me and bring him in."

Her pallor was more marked by the bright cap and shawl and the flame in her cheeks seemed scarlet.

"Hello, Harvey," she greeted him almost in her old bright voice. "Thank you for the roses. They're—"

A violent coughing made it impossible for Elsie to finish speaking.

He came and stood beside her and took her hot little outstretched hand.

"You're so pretty and I'm so glad you let me come in," he said gently.

"Oh, Harvey, I'm the one that's glad," said Elsie, trying to speak brightly. She laid back on the pillow. The effort to talk exhausted her.

Harvey knelt down beside the bed so that his face was almost on a level with hers.

"I don't want you to get tired, dear," he said. "I just want you to rest and get well. Rest now!" He put his hand tenderly on her hot forehead.

"How cool your hand feels," she murmured. "Put it over my eyes. They burn so."

He obeyed her and they remained quiet for many minutes; through their hearts went many thoughts.

She moved slightly. He understood, removed his hand and waited.

When Elsie opened her eyes she looked directly into his kind eyes filled with grief and love.

"You mustn't be so sorry for me, Harvey," she whispered.

"You will be better soon, and then—remember, little dear, I still have the wedding ring."

Elsie sighed. "Poor old Harvey! There never was anybody so good as you are to me."

"I love you."

She patted his cheek. "It's so good of you to go on caring about me."

"I couldn't stop if I wanted to,—and I don't want to."

She put her thin arm about his neck. "Will you do something for me?"

"Anything on earth!"

A wan little funny gleam lighted her pretty dark eyes.

"This is on earth, all right. I'll tell you about it next time you come...." Suddenly Elsie sat up and grasped him. "There will be a next time, won't there, Harvey?" she asked him in a wild tone, a wave of terror seeming to go over her.

He held her gently.

"Don't be frightened, dear. Of course there is going to be a next time ... all the rest of our lives. You didn't think even for a minute that I would go back on you, did you, Elsie?"

She smiled and released herself, then smiled again. "No, no, I didn't mean that. Take a chair, Harvey, and tell me about the weather."

Harvey took the chair and once more possessed himself of her hand.

She smiled sweetly.

"Now let me ask you a favor. Let's name the day, Elsie," he said. "Promise to marry me,—as soon as you get well."

"When—I—get—well," Elsie looked wonderingly at him. She saw his passionate earnestness, his need of hope. Hope! It was fast fainting in her heart. "Yes, Harvey,—when I get well."

He bent over her and with deep tenderness kissed her.

Violent coughing seized her. It was the worst, the most pro-longed Elsie had yet had. One spasm followed another, bringing her mother with remedies.

Harvey moved frantically about; he was the first to suggest the doctor and ran out to bring one. He did not realize, he could not know what had really happened.

When he returned Elsie had fallen asleep and the physician advised them not to waken her, promising to call early in the morning. The faithful Harvey went with him. He had her answer, "when I get well," she said.

Elsie remained until nearly day-break in a very deep sleep. The fever left her during this long repose. Her sister, who was watching beside her, thought she was better because her forehead grew damp and cool.

With the first early light of morning Elsie opened her eyes.

Patience pushed back the pretty tendrils of her dark hair. "It's sister watching with you, dear," she said.

"Where's mother?" murmured Elsie in a voice so weak that it frightened Patience.

"Mother! mother! Please come!" she called.

"She's coming," answered Patience as Mrs. Welcome came

hurrying to the bedside.

She understood without a word, lifting Elsie in her arms, the frail little worn body against her heart. Tears streamed down her face; sobs shook her body.

Patience hurried weeping to summon Harry.

"Don't cry, Mother," moaned Elsie. "I am so glad I am home with you."

"Yes, Elsie, yes."

"I would have come long ago, but I didn't dare—so many girls never dare go home. Some of their mothers don't want them, but you—. Mother—"

"Yes my darling, yes!"

"I was afraid, so afraid. I went—and—looked—at the—lake." She seemed to her mother to wander a bit.

Her breathing became difficult. No more words came. A few quick fluttering breaths—Elsie was gone.

CHAPTER XXXII

AT MARY RANDALL'S SUMMER HOME

Lake Geneva season was at its close. Most of the lake dwellers had closed their houses and returned to town. For those who remained late autumn had her glories. Woods and groves were gay in foliage. Orchards bowed their heads beneath their loads of ripened fruit. In shorn fields the birds, preparing for southern migration, sang of a year crowned with plenty.

Vines hung deep about the broad veranda of the villa where Mary Randall was resting from her labors in the company of her uncle and aunt. She sat alone in a corner of the veranda one sunny day, waiting for the arrival of the journalist Ambrose, one of her most efficient aids.

Anna, her faithful maid came with an armful of flowers and began arranging them on the table.

"You love those old-fashioned flowers even more than I do, I believe, Anna," said Miss Randall.

"I do love them. They seem like the blossom of my vacation," said Anna.

"That's a pretty way to put it. Your vacation is to be a good long one. You have certainly earned it. You're as worn as I am, after our battle. I never should have got through it without you."

"Thank you, Miss Mary. Here comes the flower of all your workers,—Mr. Ambrose," said the girl, and withdrew.

"Good news," said the journalist cheerfully, coming to greet his friend, and noting with a sudden swift pleasure that a faint blush came to her cheeks and a new light to her eyes as she welcomed him. "Good news! As I was coming away the newspapers were out with the extra. The city council held a special meeting during the afternoon. They have abolished the segregated district. The city has formally adopted the policy of suppressing instead of circumscribing vice."

"That is the beginning of the end," said Miss Randall. "If our campaign has won that we have won all I hoped for."

"Yet many people believe that we failed."

"Even if we had failed we should have made progress. Every movement of this kind leaves its mark on the public conscience. It makes work easier for other crusaders."

"Yes," responded Ambrose, "because it brings out the facts. Facts are lasting. They cannot die."

"Progress comes through inculcation of these facts, by means of education. Schools and churches—and parents—must concentrate on the moral improvement of the rising generation, or we wrestle ineffectively."

"The kind of vice you have been specially fighting will be extinct within the next ten years," said Ambrose. "I don't mean that we shall have suppressed vice. That is a task for centuries. But our people in the United States will not stand for this trade in girls."

"I'd like to preach to men who have daughters to protect to take their wives and go out and see some of the shady places of the city for themselves. It would make any mother far more careful in future about the companions of their daughters."

"Yes, to whisper about 'wild oats' and to see a young man who wants to marry one's daughter in a dive are two very different things."

"We are going to have vice," said Miss Randall, "as long as economic conditions set the stage for it. A young girl housed in a poor tenement, ill-lighted, poorly heated, badly ventilated, fed and clothed insufficiently—see to it that she hears foul language, and witnesses drunkenness and quarrelling—then you have the condition that produces the delinquent city girl."

"We are attacking all those evils," said Ambrose. "The public conscience is rising against them. I predict the time when it will be regarded as great a disgrace for a city to possess a 'back of the yards,' a ghetto or a slum tenement district as it is now to have a district organized for the exploitation of women. It's coming. You and I shall see it."

Mary Randall had risen, deeply moved while he spoke. She leaned against the trellis and gazed far across the silver-shot lake at the sun sinking, a great ball of crimson fire among the dark trees.

"God speed the day!" she said.

Beyond the veranda in a darkened drawing-room Mary Randall's aunt had been resting and had heard this conversation. She rose and went softly away and out to a pergola where she found her husband smoking a cigar.

"Lucius," she said. "That young newspaper man who has been out here to see Mary is here again. They are talking in the veranda, settling all the problems of Chicago!"

Lucius Randall blew a cloud of smoke. "Well, my dear, that is the only way this old world gets ahead, for each generation to tackle its problems anew."

"I believe that young man likes Mary."

"Many young men do."

"But—I really believe Mary likes him. She talks to him with a sweet note in her voice, even when they are discussing the most impossible subjects."

"I shouldn't wonder," said Lucius Randall with much serenity.

AFTERWORD

In our modern crusade against that most ancient evil known as the white slave traffic we have made at least one serious advance. All over the world that conspiracy of silence which has fettered thought and prevented open action in the fight is ended.

Nowadays, as Havelock Ellis, author of the famous "Psychology of Sex," says in the *Metropolitan* discussion of this subject, "churches, societies, journalist, legislators, have all joined the ranks of the agitators. Not only has there been no voice on the opposite side, which was scarcely to be expected—for there has never been any anxiety to cry aloud in defense of 'white slavery' from the housetops—but there has been a new and noteworthy conquest over indifference and over that sacred silence which was supposed to encompass all sexual topics with suitable darkness. The banishment of that silence in the cause of social hygiene is, indeed, not the least significant feature of this agitation. * * *

"By insuring that our workers, and especially our women workers, are decently paid, so that they can live comfortably on their wages, we shall not, indeed, have abolished prostitution, which is more than an economic phenomenon, but we shall more effectually check the white slave trader than by the most Draconic legislation the most imaginative

Virginia Brooks

vice crusader ever devised. And when we insure that these same workers have ample time and opportunity for free and joyous recreation we shall have done more to kill the fascination of the white slave traffic than by endless police regulations for the moral supervision of the young.

"No doubt the element of human nature in the manifestations we are concerned with will still be at work, an obscure instinct often acting differently in each sex, but tending to drive both into the same risks. Here we need even more fundamental social changes. It is sheer foolishness to suppose that when we raise our little dams in the path of a great stream of human impulse that stream will forthwith flow calmly back to its source. We must make our new channels concurrently with our dams. We can at least begin today a task of education which must slowly though surely undermine the white slave trader's stronghold. Such an education needs to be not merely instruction in the facts of sex and wise guidance concerning all the dangers and risks of the sexual life; it must also involve a training of the will, a development of the sense of responsibility, such as can never be secured by shutting our young people up in a hothouse, sheltered from every fortifying breath of the outside world."

It was in Illinois that Abraham Lincoln—a Southerner, Kentucky born—threw down the gage in his famous Bloomington speech in the matter of buying and selling human beings as slaves. It is in Illinois—in spite of much disgrace which the State's fair name has had forced upon it—that men and women have enlisted for life to fight in the battle against buying and selling white girls, to fight against that special dealing in "live stock" actually known to have gone on for years, which is Chicago's special shame as a distributing center.

There is eternal shouting and exhorting against the

immorality and vice of the levee, but I wonder if it isn't society's hue and cry to divert attention from viciousness in what are called "the best circles," a condition that is a hundred times more important.

Will the churches be in some measure convinced that they must organize for a combined effort to save the children of today—that souls are more important than sectarianism, and that Sunday is not the only day in the week?

If every unmarried woman with money and time at her disposal were to devote part of her leisure to the care of one child there would be far less misery in the slums and many a little sister would be saved.

If there is to be any effective reform we must arouse society from its lethargic viewpoint too generally accepted that the devil is never so black as he is painted.

As long as mothers do not know who the young men are with whom their daughters spend evenings away from home so long will there be the troop of Little Lost Sisters tripping, stumbling down the trail that leads hellward.

Let us make the war against commercialized vice a bigger thing than a presidential campaign, bigger than any war, bigger than anything that was ever known in a woman's movement before in the world!

Choose from Thousands of 1stWorldLibrary Classics By

A. M. Barnard
Ada Leverson
Adolphus William Ward
Aesop
Agatha Christie
Alexander Aaronsohn
Alexander Kielland
Alexandre Dumas
Alfred Gatty
Alfred Ollivant
Alice Duer Miller
Alice Turner Curtis
Alice Dunbar
Allen Chapman
Alleyne Ireland
Ambrose Bierce
Amelia E. Barr
Amory H. Bradford
Andrew Lang
Andrew McFarland Davis
Andy Adams
Angela Brazil
Anna Alice Chapin
Anna Sewell
Annie Besant
Annie Hamilton Donnell
Annie Payson Call
Annie Roe Carr
Annonaymous
Anton Chekhov
Archibald Lee Fletcher
Arnold Bennett
Arthur C. Benson
Arthur Conan Doyle
Arthur M. Winfield
Arthur Ransome
Arthur Schnitzler
Arthur Train
Atticus
B.H. Baden-Powell
B. M. Bower
B. C. Chatterjee
Baroness Emmuska Orczy
Baroness Orczy
Basil King
Bayard Taylor
Ben Macomber
Bertha Muzzy Bower
Bjornstjerne Bjornson

Booth Tarkington
Boyd Cable
Bram Stoker
C. Collodi
C. E. Orr
C. M. Ingleby
Carolyn Wells
Catherine Parr Traill
Charles A. Eastman
Charles Amory Beach
Charles Dickens
Charles Dudley Warner
Charles Farrar Browne
Charles Ives
Charles Kingsley
Charles Klein
Charles Hanson Towne
Charles Lathrop Pack
Charles Romyn Dake
Charles Whibley
Charles Willing Beale
Charlotte M. Braeme
Charlotte M. Yonge
Charlotte Perkins Stetson
Clair W. Hayes
Clarence Day Jr.
Clarence E. Mulford
Clemence Housman
Confucius
Coningsby Dawson
Cornelis DeWitt Wilcox
Cyril Burleigh
D. H. Lawrence
Daniel Defoe
David Garnett
Dinah Craik
Don Carlos Janes
Donald Keyhoe
Dorothy Kilner
Dougan Clark
Douglas Fairbanks
E. Nesbit
E. P. Roe
E. Phillips Oppenheim
E. S. Brooks
Earl Barnes
Edgar Rice Burroughs
Edith Van Dyne
Edith Wharton

Edward Everett Hale
Edward J. O'Biren
Edward S. Ellis
Edwin L. Arnold
Eleanor Atkins
Eleanor Hallowell Abbott
Eliot Gregory
Elizabeth Gaskell
Elizabeth McCracken
Elizabeth Von Arnim
Ellem Key
Emerson Hough
Emilie F. Carlen
Emily Bronte
Emily Dickinson
Enid Bagnold
Enilor Macartney Lane
Erasmus W. Jones
Ernie Howard Pie
Ethel May Dell
Ethel Turner
Ethel Watts Mumford
Eugene Sue
Eugenie Foa
Eugene Wood
Eustace Hale Ball
Evelyn Everett-green
Everard Cotes
F. H. Cheley
F. J. Cross
F. Marion Crawford
Fannie E. Newberry
Federick Austin Ogg
Ferdinand Ossendowski
Fergus Hume
Florence A. Kilpatrick
Fremont B. Deering
Francis Bacon
Francis Darwin
Frances Hodgson Burnett
Frances Parkinson Keyes
Frank Gee Patchin
Frank Harris
Frank Jewett Mather
Frank L. Packard
Frank V. Webster
Frederic Stewart Isham
Frederick Trevor Hill
Frederick Winslow Taylor

Friedrich Kerst
Friedrich Nietzsche
Fyodor Dostoyevsky
G.A. Henty
G.K. Chesterton
Gabrielle E. Jackson
Garrett P. Serviss
Gaston Leroux
George A. Warren
George Ade
Geroge Bernard Shaw
George Cary Eggleston
George Durston
George Ebers
George Eliot
George Gissing
George MacDonald
George Meredith
George Orwell
George Sylvester Viereck
George Tucker
George W. Cable
George Wharton James
Gertrude Atherton
Gordon Casserly
Grace E. King
Grace Gallatin
Grace Greenwood
Grant Allen
Guillermo A. Sherwell
Gulielma Zollinger
Gustav Flaubert
H. A. Cody
H. B. Irving
H. C. Bailey
H. G. Wells
H. H. Munro
H. Irving Hancock
H. R. Naylor
H. Rider Haggard
H. W. C. Davis
Haldeman Julius
Hall Caine
Hamilton Wright Mabie
Hans Christian Andersen
Harold Avery
Harold McGrath
Harriet Beecher Stowe
Harry Castlemon
Harry Coghill
Harry Houidini

Hayden Carruth
Helent Hunt Jackson
Helen Nicolay
Hendrik Conscience
Hendy David Thoreau
Henri Barbusse
Henrik Ibsen
Henry Adams
Henry Ford
Henry Frost
Henry James
Henry Jones Ford
Henry Seton Merriman
Henry W Longfellow
Herbert A. Giles
Herbert Carter
Herbert N. Casson
Herman Hesse
Hildegard G. Frey
Homer
Honore De Balzac
Horace B. Day
Horace Walpole
Horatio Alger Jr.
Howard Pyle
Howard R. Garis
Hugh Lofting
Hugh Walpole
Humphry Ward
Ian Maclaren
Inez Haynes Gillmore
Irving Bacheller
Isabel Cecilia Williams
Isabel Hornibrook
Israel Abrahams
Ivan Turgenev
J. G.Austin
J. Henri Fabre
J. M. Barrie
J. M. Walsh
J. Macdonald Oxley
J. R. Miller
J. S. Fletcher
J. S. Knowles
J. Storer Clouston
J. W. Duffield
Jack London
Jacob Abbott
James Allen
James Andrews
James Baldwin

James Branch Cabell
James DeMille
James Joyce
James Lane Allen
James Lane Allen
James Oliver Curwood
James Oppenheim
James Otis
James R. Driscoll
Jane Abbott
Jane Austen
Jane L. Stewart
Janet Aldridge
Jens Peter Jacobsen
Jerome K. Jerome
Jessie Graham Flower
John Buchan
John Burroughs
John Cournos
John F. Kennedy
John Gay
John Glasworthy
John Habberton
John Joy Bell
John Kendrick Bangs
John Milton
John Philip Sousa
John Taintor Foote
Jonas Lauritz Idemil Lie
Jonathan Swift
Joseph A. Altsheler
Joseph Carey
Joseph Conrad
Joseph E. Badger Jr
Joseph Hergesheimer
Joseph Jacobs
Jules Vernes
Julian Hawthrone
Julie A Lippmann
Justin Huntly McCarthy
Kakuzo Okakura
Karle Wilson Baker
Kate Chopin
Kenneth Grahame
Kenneth McGaffey
Kate Langley Bosher
Kate Langley Bosher
Katherine Cecil Thurston
Katherine Stokes
L. A. Abbot
L. T. Meade

L. Frank Baum
Latta Griswold
Laura Dent Crane
Laura Lee Hope
Laurence Housman
Lawrence Beasley
Leo Tolstoy
Leonid Andreyev
Lewis Carroll
Lewis Sperry Chafer
Lilian Bell
Lloyd Osbourne
Louis Hughes
Louis Joseph Vance
Louis Tracy
Louisa May Alcott
Lucy Fitch Perkins
Lucy Maud Montgomery
Luther Benson
Lydia Miller Middleton
Lyndon Orr
M. Corvus
M. H. Adams
Margaret E. Sangster
Margret Howth
Margaret Vandercook
Margaret W. Hungerford
Margret Penrose
Maria Edgeworth
Maria Thompson Daviess
Mariano Azuela
Marion Polk Angellotti
Mark Overton
Mark Twain
Mary Austin
Mary Catherine Crowley
Mary Cole
Mary Hastings Bradley
Mary Roberts Rinehart
Mary Rowlandson
M. Wollstonecraft Shelley
Maud Lindsay
Max Beerbohm
Myra Kelly
Nathaniel Hawthrone
Nicolo Machiavelli
O. F. Walton
Oscar Wilde
Owen Johnson
P.G. Wodehouse
Paul and Mabel Thorne

Paul G. Tomlinson
Paul Severing
Percy Brebner
Percy Keese Fitzhugh
Peter B. Kyne
Plato
Quincy Allen
R. Derby Holmes
R. L. Stevenson
R. S. Ball
Rabindranath Tagore
Rahul Alvares
Ralph Bonehill
Ralph Henry Barbour
Ralph Victor
Ralph Waldo Emmerson
Rene Descartes
Ray Cummings
Rex Beach
Rex E. Beach
Richard Harding Davis
Richard Jefferies
Richard Le Gallienne
Robert Barr
Robert Frost
Robert Gordon Anderson
Robert L. Drake
Robert Lansing
Robert Lynd
Robert Michael Ballantyne
Robert W. Chambers
Rosa Nouchette Carey
Rudyard Kipling
Saint Augustine
Samuel B. Allison
Samuel Hopkins Adams
Sarah Bernhardt
Sarah C. Hallowell
Selma Lagerlof
Sherwood Anderson
Sigmund Freud
Standish O'Grady
Stanley Weyman
Stella Benson
Stella M. Francis
Stephen Crane
Stewart Edward White
Stijn Streuvels
Swami Abhedananda
Swami Parmananda
T. S. Ackland

T. S. Arthur
The Princess Der Ling
Thomas A. Janvier
Thomas A Kempis
Thomas Anderton
Thomas Bailey Aldrich
Thomas Bulfinch
Thomas De Quincey
Thomas Dixon
Thomas H. Huxley
Thomas Hardy
Thomas More
Thornton W. Burgess
U. S. Grant
Upton Sinclair
Valentine Williams
Various Authors
Vaughan Kester
Victor Appleton
Victor G. Durham
Victoria Cross
Virginia Woolf
Wadsworth Camp
Walter Camp
Walter Scott
Washington Irving
Wilbur Lawton
Wilkie Collins
Willa Cather
Willard F. Baker
William Dean Howells
William le Queux
W. Makepeace Thackeray
William W. Walter
William Shakespeare
Winston Churchill
Yei Theodora Ozaki
Yogi Ramacharaka
Young E. Allison
Zane Grey